Toy Making

Toy Making

Gladys and Kathryn Greenaway

DRAKE PUBLISHERS INC

New York

ISBN 0-87749-563-7

Library of Congress Catalog Card Number 73-10902

Published in 1974 by
Drake Publishers Inc
381 Park Avenue South
New York, N. Y. 10016

Printed in Great Britain

Contents

Illustrations

PATTERNS

Introducing Soft Toys

Playthings are important in every child's life from the moment their little fingers begin to grip and their eyes to look round. They learn through them. Learn to feel and explore, to look and to love.

In the early days their world is small and they need toys they can grasp easily – to say nothing of sucking and chewing them!

Sometimes I think the children of parents who have little money to spare are far better off than those of parents who can afford to buy anything the parents want! Some toys bought for small children are frustrating and idiotic – for instance, the enormous teddy-bear sometimes bought for a tiny child. This is almost frightening in its size and far too big to be cuddled. Some expensive toys are beautifully made but downright silly. A huge and expensive panda was given to a sharp little two year old I know – I would have loved it! There was a long zip down the back, reasonably hidden by its soft fur. For the life of me I can't think why it was there in the first place unless it was so that the stuffing could be taken out for washing. As the stuffing consisted of foam plastic granules it would have washed along with the panda!

The toddler was left alone with her new pet. All was quiet and her parents were congratulating themselves and thinking how happy it was making her. Going back to the nursery they discovered why. She had managed to undo the zip and was happily throwing foam plastic granules everywhere. The lovely panda was a limp, sad ghost of what he had been. They were able to re-stuff the poor thing but the mess was indescribable. Fortunately the child had not tried eating the pretty pieces.

The big joke was that someone else had given the child a teddy-bear knitted from scraps of wool. She adored it and took it to bed every night. If it couldn't be found there were ructions. Unfortunately the person who made it had stuffed it with kapok and rather loosely, too. Even before it was washed it became limp, but after washing it went as flat as a board.

Parents often buy toys because they like them and think how much they would like to have had them when they were young – or because large and expensive toys are a status symbol. Young children, however, have no knowledge of money or status symbols and only want something to love and cuddle.

A child will often turn from an expensive toy to an old, disreputable rag doll and hug it lovingly. It is amazing how a toy which you think will amuse a child for a short time can become a constant companion for years.

The idea that boys should not have a doll to play with because it may make them 'sissy' is fortunately outdated. Sensible people now realise that boys need something to love and cuddle just as much as girls. One of my own grandsons amused me immensely by telling me that his younger brother would like me to make him a doll. He then qualified the remark by saying he would like one himself. Both boys were already at school and, believe me, far from 'sissies'. In fact, they are tough little eggs. Both toys were made out of odd balls of wool left over from other things. When the boys are tired from their more boisterous efforts with guns and tanks and making the house hideous with raucous yells, they will settle down with the soft toys I have made them over the years and play schools. Even a couple of woollen hedgehogs are drawn into the fun.

Materials for soft toys can be culled from the rag-bag – or, if you don't happen to have anything so old-fashioned, bought at the remnant counter. Most large stores have them. One of the first soft toys I made was from the legs of old gym stockings. My older son loved it dearly and wherever he went his 'friend' went with him, usually held by one arm.

The best of old garments can be used. The new nylon velvet is excellent for dogs and cats and easier to work with than fur fabric although some toys do need this for the best results. Strong cotton material is excellent as it is easy to work with and the colours are usually gay.

Whatever material you are using it should first be washed, even if new. This ensures that it is not only clean but preshrunk, and that any surplus dye has been washed out. If the material doesn't stand up to washing it is useless.

Stuffing is very important. Kapok, as I have already said, quickly goes lumpy and cannot be washed. At one time it was possible to buy washable stuffing but this seems to have gone off the market, even in a store which specializes in toy-making equipment; anyway, it was always rather expensive. I tried using foam plastic granules but this was not very satisfactory. Although light-weight and washable, the 'nodules' spoiled the smooth appearance unless the material was very thick, such as fur fabric or tweed.

For a time I used it with finely shredded nylon but recently I have heard a horrifying story. There have been several cases in which furniture has been stuffed with plastic foam, and when left near heat this has 'exploded'. At the time of writing there has not been sufficient scientific research into the cause but it is thought possible that the plastic gives off an inflammable vapour when placed near heat. There was a case of a chair 'exploding' when standing two feet away from a gas fire and a small boy was severely burnt. So, whether or not it is safe to use plastic filling in conjunction with other filling, I don't intend to use it again until a great deal more research is done. Children's toys must be absolutely safe.

I never throw away nylon. Tights, stockings and underclothes are washed and stored away to be cut up in spare moments. I beg old nylon garments from my friends – I haven't yet taken to stealing! The nylon has to be cut into small pieces and this is rather a chore. If you do not do this the result is a lumpy toy. When wire is used for a base the nylon is cut into long strips for binding. It is easy to cut the nylon on to a sheet of paper and then store it away in a bag.

The advantage of this stuffing is that the animal or doll can even be put in the washing-machine when grubby and, after a blow on the line, will come up almost like new.

Make toys that are designed for wear, tear and loving, if sometimes rough, usage. By all means teach children to be gentle but don't expect too much of them. Such toys cost little to make and give hours of fun.

This book has been written so that those who have never made a toy in their lives can have a shot at it and gradually become more proficient. The toys are graded from the simplest to the more complicated. The book has also been designed so that once you have the basic pattern you can begin to use your own ideas, altering patterns and, after a time, designing your own.

Equipment is minimal. A sewing-machine is an asset but not absolutely necessary although it is not only quicker to sew a seam on a machine but stronger. A pair of sharp scissors is a necessity. Wire-cutters and pliers are needed for toys which have a wire frame. A knitting-needle with a large round head is useful for pushing stuffing into arms and legs, and one with a smaller head for tips of ears and tails. A long screwdriver was used for stuffing part of the monkey.

Although felt is an easy material to work with it has been used sparingly as it is not washable.

For those who enjoy knitting some patterns for these toys are included.

Toys are not only fun to make for your children or grandchildren but sell like hot cakes at bazaars and 'sales of work'.

Special Note

The majority of the patterns in this book are full size and can be traced exactly as they appear. Where reduction has been necessary the graph method has been used, each square representing 1 in. × 1 in. on the full-size pattern. It is thus a simple matter to project a full-size pattern from the pattern reproduced in the book. Just prepare your own 1 in. × 1 in. grid and draw in the pattern to correspond with the one in the book.

Chapter 1

Ball-Cat-Baby Bunny-Puppy

BALL

For pattern (to full scale) see page 12

MATERIALS

This can be made of velvet, printed cotton or fine woollen cloth. Do not mix materials. If one section is made of velvet and another of cotton or wool the sections will 'pull' and the finished product be out of shape when it is stuffed. So: all cotton, all velvet or all wool. For each section you will need a piece of material about seven inches by three. The ball is made in six sections.

Nylon for stuffing.

METHOD

Cut all sections on the straight of the material. Even if only slightly on the cross they will pull out of shape.

Tack the pieces together on the wrong side and then stitch firmly. Join first and last section together leaving about three inches open for stuffing.

Turn right side out and stuff. Do not put in too much stuffing at a time. Small amounts pushed well in is the answer to success. Stuff tightly.

Turn in the edges of the opening and oversew with tiny stitches. The new 'invisible' nylon thread is excellent for all finishing but never use a long thread with this as it is inclined to tangle. Should the ball be slightly 'lumpy' it may not have been stuffed evenly. This is why it is important that all toys are stuffed a little at a time.

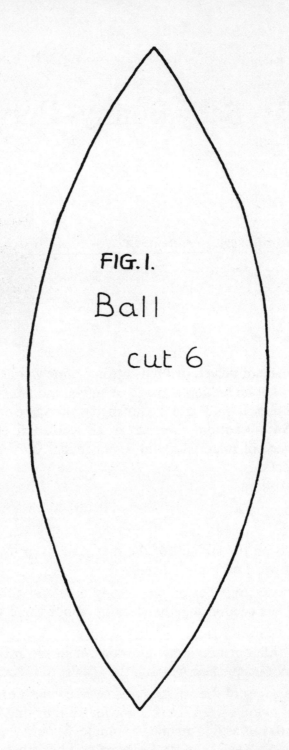

FIG. I.

Ball

cut 6

CAT

For pattern (to full scale) see pages 14–15

MATERIALS

About half a yard of thirty-six-inch material. Velvet, fine wool, checked or flowered cotton or fine tweed.

Small piece of cotton or felt for face.

Embroidery thread.

Cord for tail.

Stuffing.

METHOD

This is a very simple toy to make consisting of three main pieces. No pattern is given for the tail as this is just a straight strip of material about two and a half to three inches wide and any length you wish. If velvet is to be used it is important that the pile brushes downwards at front and back. This toy can also be used as a doorstop. If it is, for this you will also need a round piece of wood about ten inches long, a piece of fairly flexible cardboard and some pebbles. In this case the cat is improved by using a sequin in the centre of the pupils to give a sparkle. Instructions for doorstop are given in brackets.

For a child's toy it is better to make the face of fawn or cream cotton rather than felt as it may need frequent washing. Cut all pieces. The features can either be traced on to the cotton or felt or copied. If no tracing-paper is available greaseproof paper can be used, although not so good. When transferring the features on to the material use embroidery carbon or the best carbon paper. Cheap carbon paper smears. If using

FIG.2. Cat

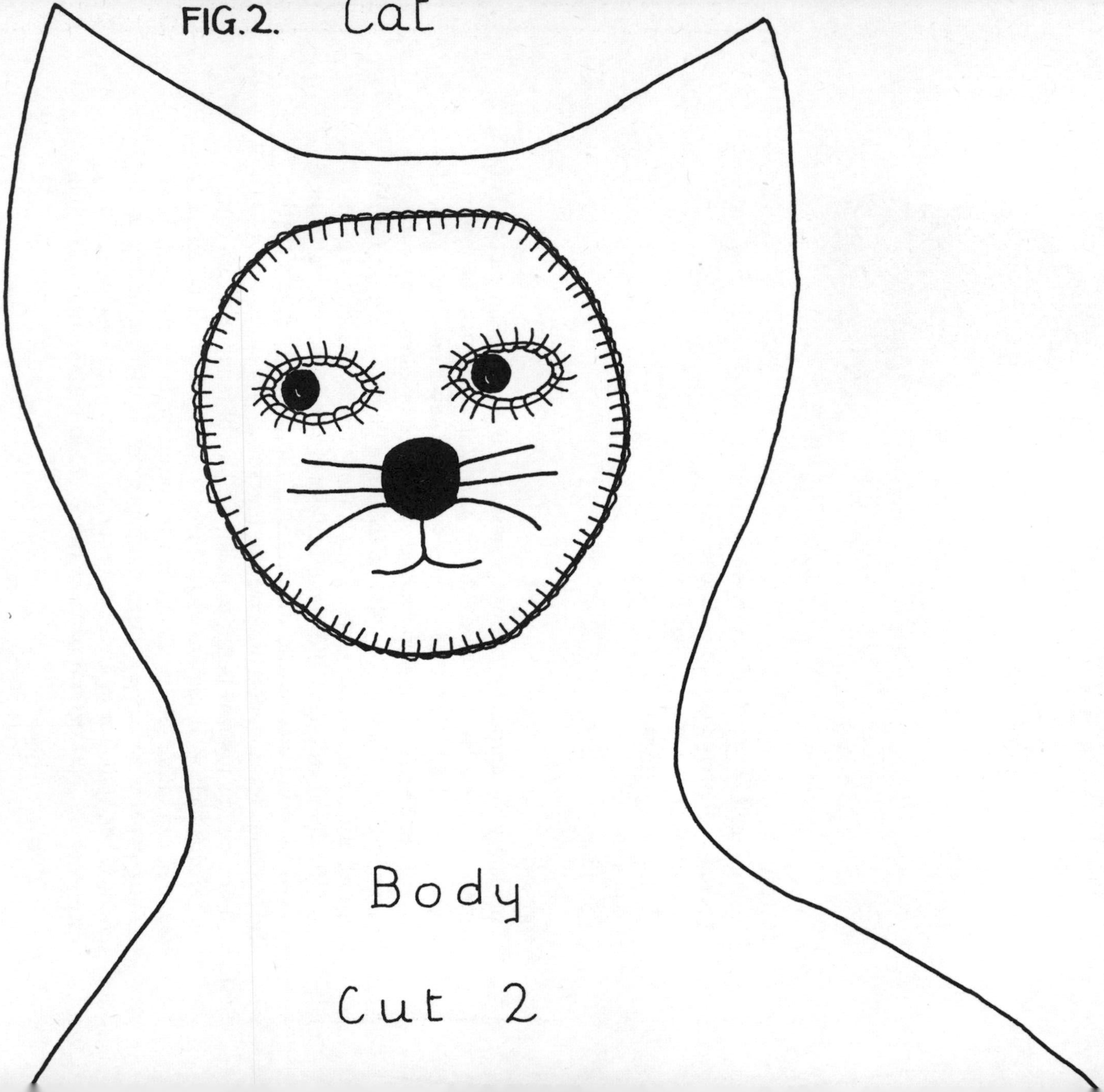

Body

Cut 2

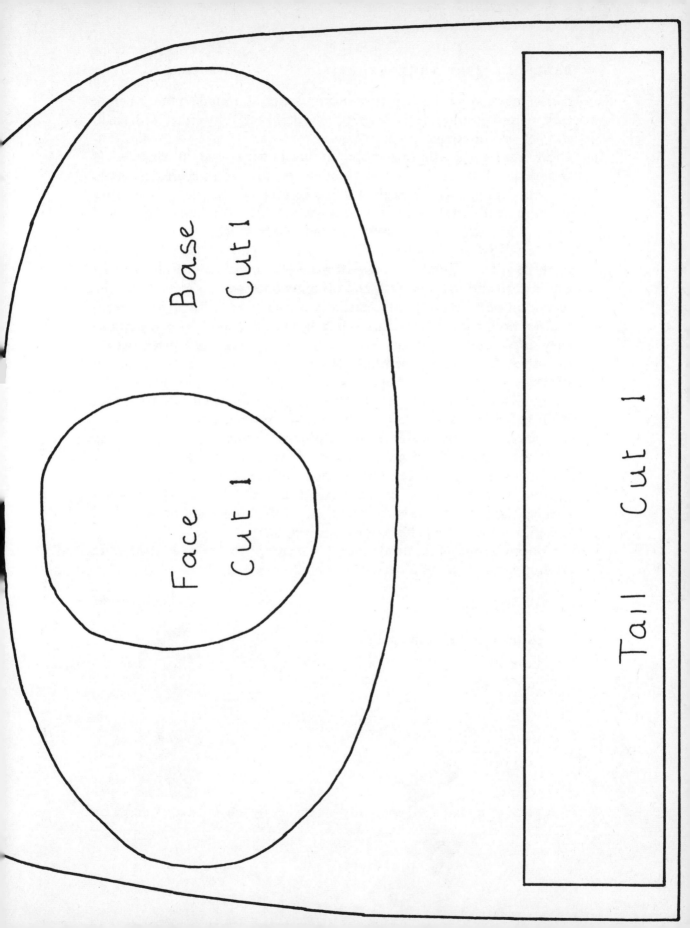

Base
Cut 1

Face
Cut 1

Tail   Cut 1

cotton material for the face, turn in a tiny edge all round and tack before tacking into position on the head. Stitch round carefully either with small stitches or buttonhole-stitch.

Embroider the elliptical pupil in black with straight stitches. If stranded cotton is used no more than two or three strands are necessary. Surround pupils with straight stitches in green or blue. The eyelashes are made with straight stitches in black. Straight stitches for nose and mouth. The whiskers are embroidered in stem-stitch.

The tail is made by hand. Cut cord about two inches shorter than material for tail. Fold one edge of material in and tack. Roll material round cord and tack into position, bringing one end to a point. Hem the turned-in edge securely with matching cotton or invisible nylon thread.

Place both parts of body face to face and tack securely. This is particularly important when using velvet as the pile 'pushes' one piece against the other. Machine or sew round securely. Tack base into position and stitch, leaving a four-inch opening at the back. Turn right side out.

Put in a small quantity of stuffing and push this well into the head. With the ball end of a long knitting-needle push the stuffing well into the ears so that they stand stiffly. Continue stuffing head.

(If for a doorstop insert the piece of wood when the head is half stuffed. Make sure it is central and then stuff all round it carefully. The stuffing must be packed in tightly. Cut a piece of cardboard slightly smaller than the base and roll it; then push it into the opening and flatten, adding some pebbles for extra weight.)

Continue stuffing cat firmly. Sew tail inside at centre back. Add more stuffing if necessary and oversew opening.

BABY BUNNY

For pattern (to full scale) see pages 18–19

MATERIALS

A piece of material either twenty-six inches by ten, or twenty inches by thirteen. Cotton or fine wool may be used but velvet is the most suitable. This must be cut so that the pile brushes downwards both back and front.

Embroidery thread for features.

Small amount of nylon stuffing as the animal must be very soft.

Ears may be lined with the same material or contrast.

METHOD

Cut all pieces. Trace face and embroider. Make darts in head. Place two main pieces right sides together and stitch round leaving opening at one side for stuffing. Turn right side out. Stuff lightly.

Stitch round ears on wrong side and turn right side out, then turn in bottom edges and oversew.

Sew ears on head, curving outer edges to front as in Plate 1. This toy is particularly suitable for a baby as it is easy to grasp.

PUPPY

For pattern (to full scale) see pages 20–21

This toy is a little more complicated than the cat as it has front paws and separate ears.

MATERIALS

It takes very little material, less than half a yard. Gaily coloured cotton, soft wool or velvet can be used. The dog in Plate 1 was made from a piece of an old velvet curtain. If you use velvet make sure the pile brushes either downwards from the centre back, or back from nose to tail.

A small piece of lining is needed for the ears. Silk is better with velvet. These can be made to stand up if wished by cutting an inch shorter at the base and cutting to a point instead of round. In this case a piece of interlining in stiff cotton is necessary.

17

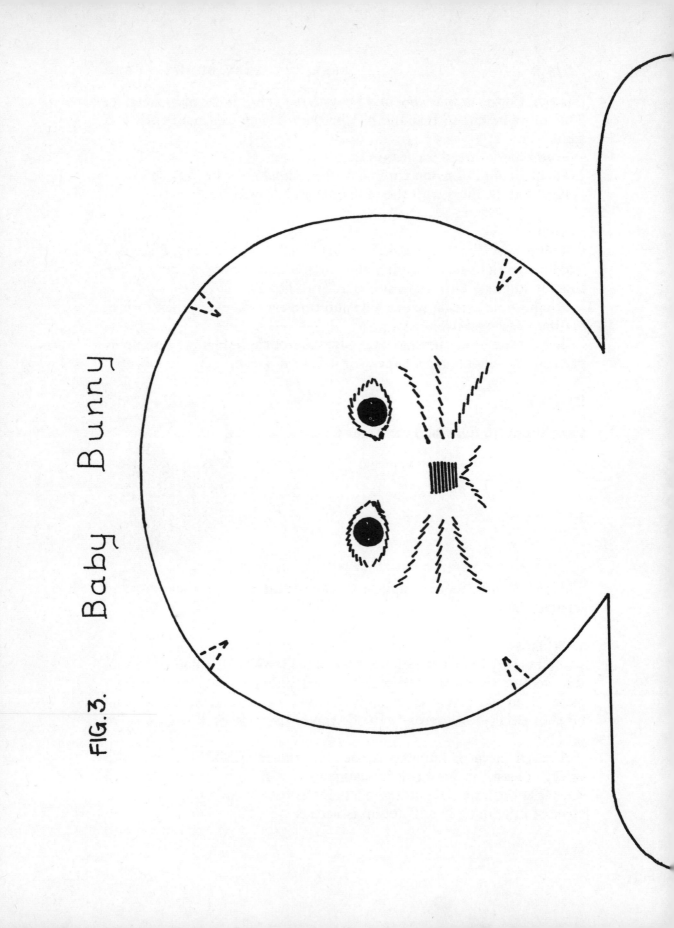

FIG. 3.   Baby   Bunny

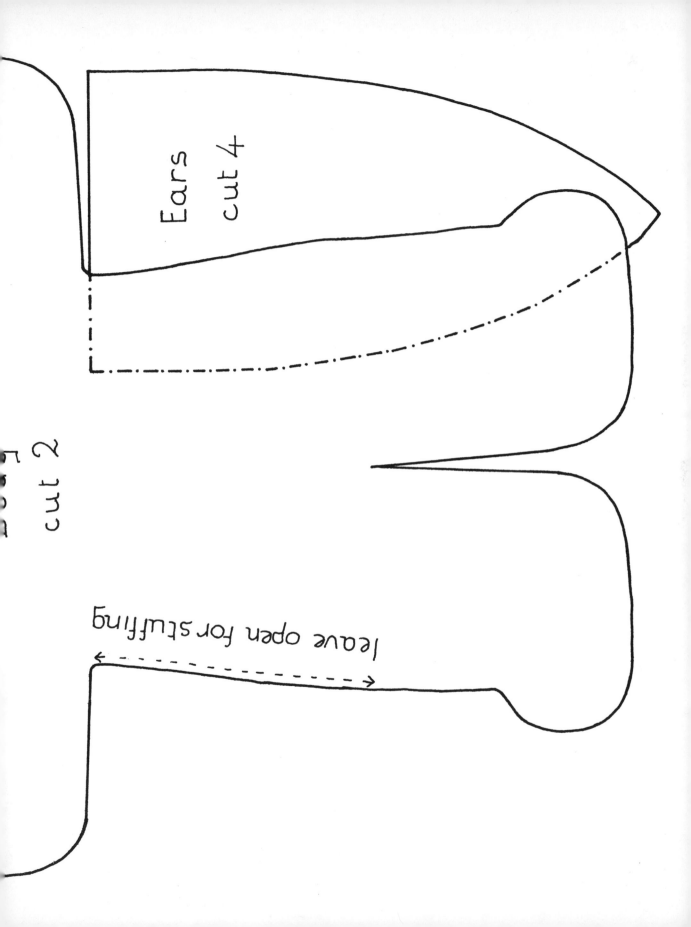

Ears
cut 4

Body
cut 2

leave open for stuffing

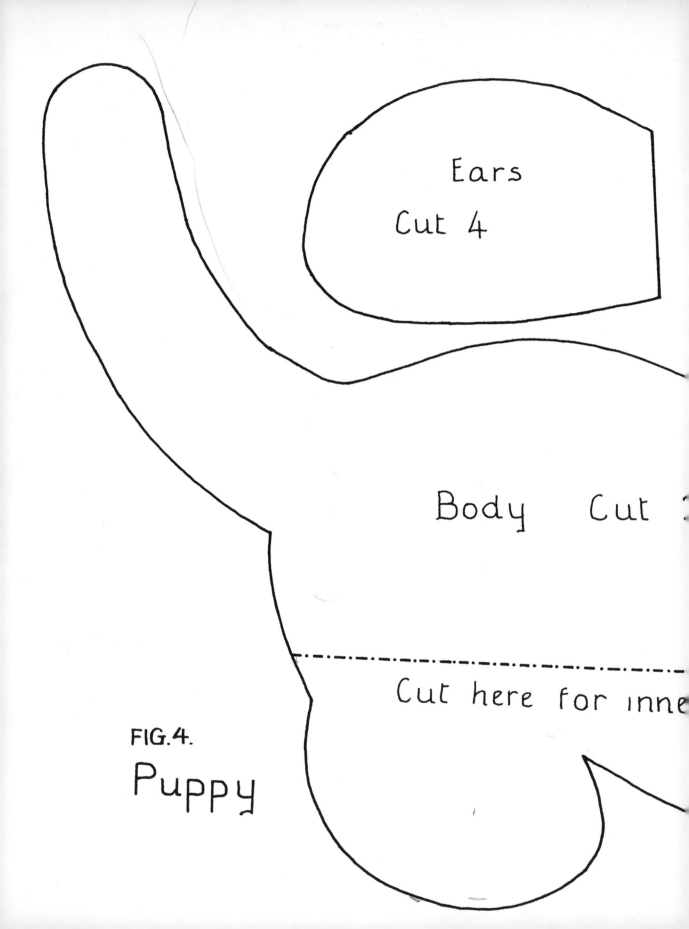

Ears

Cut 4

Body   Cut ?

Cut here for inne

FIG.4.

Puppy

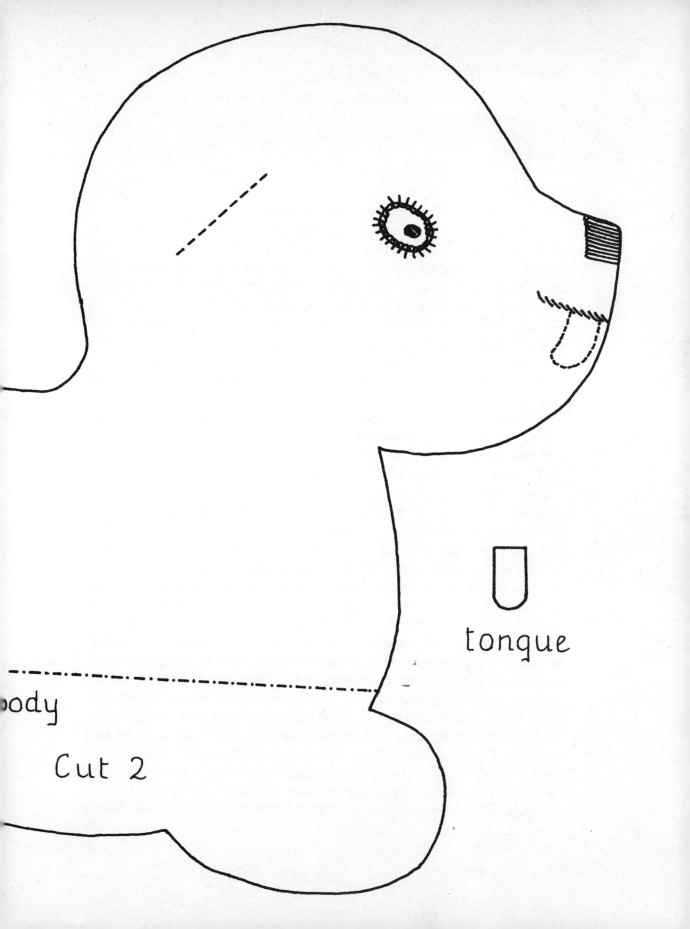

tonque

ody

Cut 2

Two buttons about a half an inch in diameter were used for the eyes but they can be embroidered.

A few inches of braid or ribbon for collar.

Stuffing.

METHOD

Cut two pieces for upper body, one for lower.

Place right sides of upper body together and tack from cross marked at neck on pattern, round head and over back and round tail. Tacking should be about a quarter of an inch inside cut edge. Sew or machine inside tacking. The upper paws are slightly wider than lower so make a running-stitch round them and gather slightly to fit.

Tack lower body to upper from cross marked on under-body to cross at tail end. Do the same on the other side and turn right side out. There are now two openings. Tail end is for stuffing. The opening at the neck must be turned in and oversewn carefully. If it is done on the wrong side it is inclined to pucker. Invisible nylon thread is better if using velvet. If using cotton or woollen material it is easier to use a matching cotton.

Cut two ears of main material and two of lining. Stitch on wrong side and turn right side out.

Stitch ears into place along line marked on pattern.

Now stuff the dog, starting with the tail and pushing the stuffing well in with the ball end of a knitting-needle so that the tail stands firmly. Now stuff head and work back along body using small amounts of stuffing at a time. Oversew opening.

With a long needle and button or embroidery thread sew the eyes in position. Make a knot on the thread and pass it right through the head from one eye position to the other and put on the first button. Pass the needle through the second hole on the button and back through the head and put on the second button. Bring the thread back through the second button to the first and repeat. Do not draw the thread too tight in either case. Make sure the two buttons are sewn strongly in position and then pass the thread over and over the 'holding' thread of the button to make a pupil, pass the thread through again and do the same with the other eye. The thread is now pushed through the hole in the button and secured under it. This is not as tricky as it sounds providing you make sure the eye of the needle is only just large enough to take the thread. Too large an eye may be difficult to get through the holes of the buttons.

Using either three strands of stranded embroidery thread or button thread, make a large cross on the nose and then use satin-stitch to complete it. The paws are finished with four black stitches. If using ribbon for round the neck, make a neat bow and sew into position. If using braid a bow is unnecessary. Just fold it over and stitch. A piece of gold braid makes a very elegant finish.

Chapter 2

Octopus-Woolly Top-Leopard

OCTOPUS

MATERIAL

This is just a two-ounce hank of wool of any colour.
A piece of felt for the hat.
Ribbon to tie tentacles.
Embroidery thread of fine wool for the features.
A circle of material and a little stuffing for the head.

METHOD (*no pattern necessary*)

Cut a circle of material of about nine inches in diameter. Any material will do but it should match the wool as closely as possible. Make a running-stitch round the edge with strong cotton and gather it up leaving a space for stuffing. Stuff firmly then draw up opening and finish off tightly.

Sew one end of hank to top of ball and arrange wool all round so that it is completely covered; secure round 'neck' with strong cotton and stitch firmly.

Cut the ends of the hank and divide into eight equal parts. Plait each part and secure the ends. Embroider features. Tie a bow of ribbon at the end of each tentacle and round neck. The hat can be made of a flat circle of felt with a bow on top or two triangles stitched on two sides to make a cocked hat. This can be finished with a tiny feather.

24

WOOLLY TOP

This doll is about ten inches high but the size can be altered according to the materials at hand. Black wool was used but dark brown is just as attractive. In the latter case the base would also be brown.

MATERIALS

A piece of black material seven and a half inches by six.

Two ounces of cheap, 4-ply black wool.

Odd lengths of any brightly coloured wool for skirt and necklace.

Small amount of stuffing.

Four pieces of cardboard for winding wool: eleven and a half inches long for head, body and legs. Eight and a half inches long and four inches wide for arms. An inch deep and four inches wide for hair. Four inches deep and six inches wide for skirt.

METHOD (*no pattern necessary*)

Fold material widthwise. Round top of head, leaving bottom straight. Stitch round sides and head, leaving bottom open. Stuff very tightly for about two inches. Run draw thread round, pull very tightly and fasten to form neck. Linen thread is needed for this. Stuff body and sew up end.

Make the arms first by winding the wool evenly but not too tightly round the eight-and-a-half-inch cardboard. This will take about half an ounce of wool. Oversew wool at centre of cardboard at back and front. Without cutting, slide wool off cardboard. Slip this hank of wool over head of doll and down to shoulders. Stitch firmly back and front and cut loops at end.

With ball of wool stitch one end firmly to shoulder and then wind carefully round arm of doll, keeping the binding even. The success of this doll lies in the careful binding. Tighten binding for wrist and loosen again for hand. Separate wool into five pieces for fingers and thumb. When hand is partly bound make thumb by taking wool to end of pieces

[*continued on p. 28*]

FIG.5. Leopard

Flower Necklace

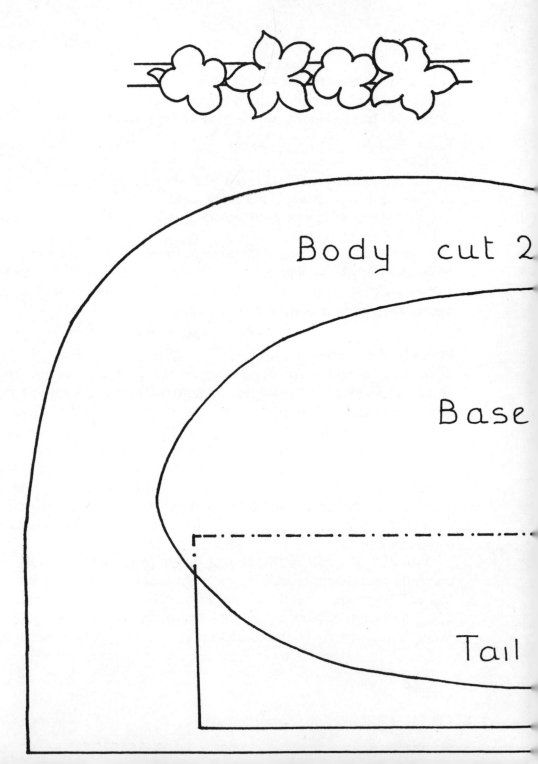

Body   cut 2

Base

Tail

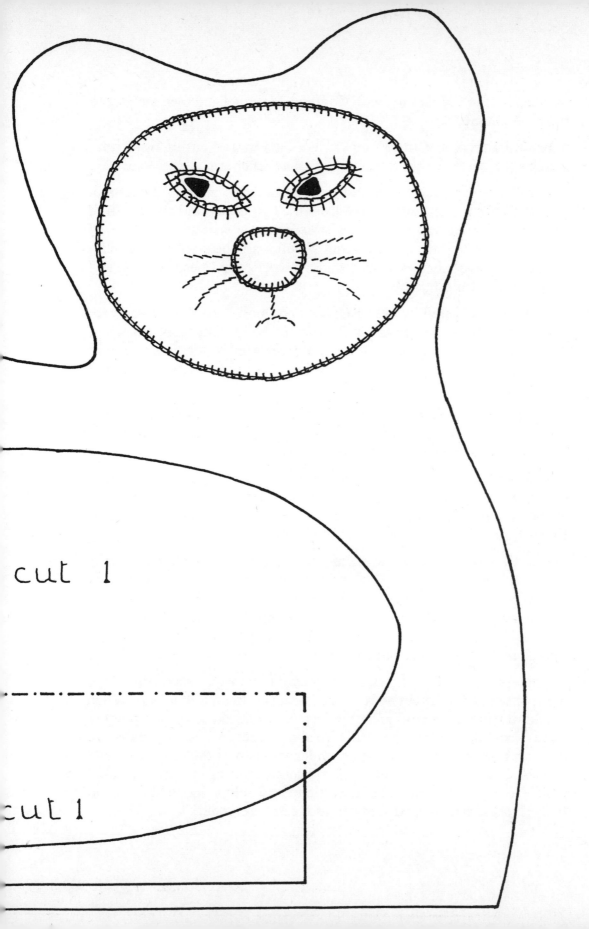

cut 1

cut 1

for thumb, binding back to hand. Continue binding hand then make each finger as thumb.

Break off wool and thread on needle. Pass in and out of hand until secure then cut end close to hand. Complete other arm in the same way.

Wind wool for head, body and legs on the large piece of cardboard. This will take the rest of the wool from the first ounce and about half of the second. When you have wound this, oversew one end and slide off cardboard. Place sewn end on head of doll, half the wool in front and half at back and stitch in place. Arrange wool round head to neck and tie securely with thread.

Arrange wool carefully over body. Do not bind head. Bind body with wool as for arms. Fasten off at bottom of body. Cut wool evenly at bottom and separate for legs. Bind these as for arms, tighten a little at ankles and bring the wool at angle for feet. Fasten off by sewing in and out under feet.

The eyes are made with six small stitches of white wool in the form of a triangle, with a couple of black stitches in the centre. The mouth is made with four stitches of red wool.

Bind wool round inch-deep cardboard for hair but not too much at a time. Oversew wool at one side. Slide wool off cardboard and arrange on head, stitching firmly into place. Continue until head is covered. Loops may now be cut and trimmed into shape.

The skirt is made by winding any pieces of coloured wool on to the four-inch-deep cardboard. The brighter and more varied the colours the better. Stitch this along one side as for hair and slide off cardboard. If it is not sufficient to go round the doll you can make another piece. Sew this on to the doll and cut the ends to form 'grass' skirt. The necklace is made with a plait of bright wool.

This is a very soft doll but it is very easy to wire it. To do this take a piece of wire about twenty-two inches long and bend into a loop. When you have stuffed the head push the loop of wire up through the body to neck. Now take another piece of wire about eight inches long and push through body at shoulders, pass it under the loop of the other wire and out through the other shoulder. Bend loops at ends of wire and bind arms and legs with strips of nylon, stitching firmly at loops of wire and body. Now stuff body and continue as for unwired doll.

28

LEOPARD

For pattern (to full scale) see pages 26–27

Once you have made the cat the leopard is simple. Materials required are the same but you will need more stuffing. The one in Plate 2 was made with pieces left over from a 'leopard' pattern cotton housecoat. The only addition is a bunch of golden-brown wool sewn into the end of the tail instead of bringing it to a point. This is made by winding the wool round four fingers, sewing it into the tail and then cutting the loops. If it is to be used for a doorstop the piece of wood is not necessary, just the cardboard and pebbles at base.

Follow instructions as for cat.

This toy makes an equally good lion with the addition of a mane. For a very smart lion golden-brown velvet is excellent. The mane is made of golden-brown wool wound round a piece of cardboard about two and a half inches wide and nine or ten inches long. Wind wool round and round smoothly until the card is covered and then oversew at one edge. Cut other edge carefully with a sharp knife or scissors and arrange in rows round head of lion.

Chapter 3

Madam Gonk-Lion Glove Puppet-Baby Lamb

Gonks and Weirdies can be made from almost any material and of any size. The main thing is to let your imagination run riot. Little children love them and sometimes an older girl will think them great fun to 'decorate' her bedroom or to sit on her bed much as, a few years ago, it was fashionable to have a beautifully-made lion or poodle. Perhaps 'gonks' go with the alteration in the style of dress! The pattern provided can be altered a great deal by being made narrower or taller according to the amount of material to hand.

MADAM GONK

For pattern (reduced scale) see pages 32–33 and pattern for clothes (full scale) see pages 34–35

MATERIALS

Third of a yard of thirty-six-inch heavy 'slub' silk in pale blue.
A piece of natural coloured felt for hands.
Tiny pieces of red, black and white felt for features.
Pieces left over from the hands were used for nose and irises.

Voile, four inches deep and nine inches wide for apron. Narrow lace to trim.

About twenty inches of four-inch-wide lace to go round hands. All lace used was unpicked from an old nylon slip.

About five inches of inch to an inch-and-a-half wide material for apron band.

Ribbon to tie round waist.

About an ounce of carpet wool was used for the hair which was made into a wig on a firm base and sewn on after 'Madam' was finished.

This toy needs a lot of stuffing.

Four pieces of cardboard for winding wool. Each piece about five or six inches long and in depths of one and a half inches, two inches, two and a half inches and three inches.

METHOD

Cut all pieces and stitch darts as in Fig. 6. Sew on features with tiny stitches. The eyes can be made to look straight ahead, sideways or even given a 'squint'.

Stitch hands close to edges on right sides and stuff lightly.

Cut wide lace in half and gather a piece round each hand and tack securely. Place right sides of body together, putting the hands inside. Pin the wrists just below the curve of the shoulders then tack all round the gonk carefully, making sure the lace as well as the hands are sewn into the seam. Stitch round leaving bottom open for stuffing. Turn right side out. The hands should stand out from the body. Stuff very firmly and sew up bottom. Place upper and lower parts of feet right sides together and stitch round heel and outer sides and toes leaving a couple of inches open on the inner sides for stuffing. Turn right sides out and stuff firmly. Sew up opening. Stitch feet to base about an inch and a half apart.

Hem apron round sides and bottom and trim with frills of lace. Gather into five-inch band and sew on ribbon ties.

The wig.   Make darts in wig base and stitch flat. Turn in edge all round and stitch. Wind wool smoothly along narrowest cardboard, single winding only. With needle and cotton to match wool oversew loops together on one side. Slip off card but do not cut loops until later. Stitch on to base where you see dotted line on Fig. 7. Wind wool on two-inch card and repeat on second row of fringe. Again using the narrow card wind and oversew then make the first row of hair at back of wig. Repeat

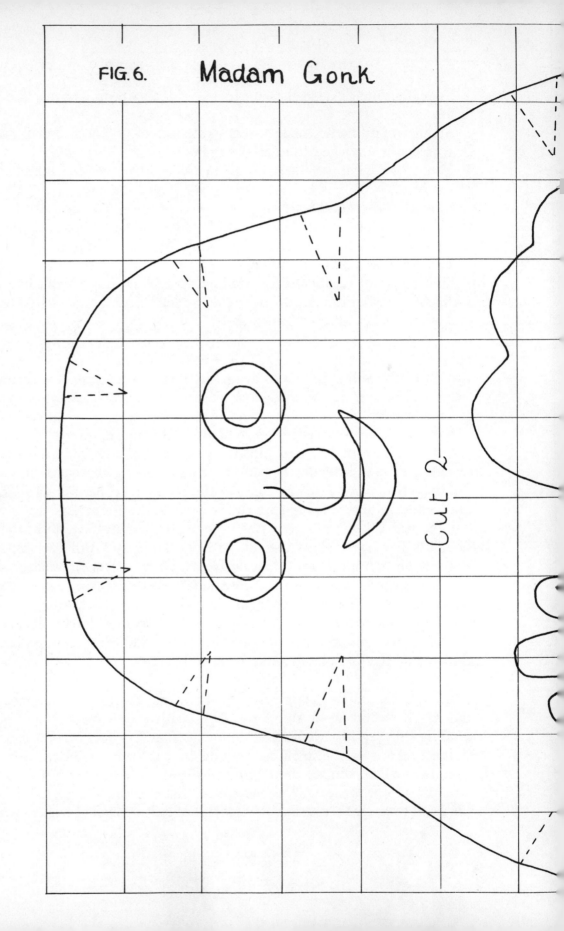

FIG. 6.   Madam Gonk

Cut 2

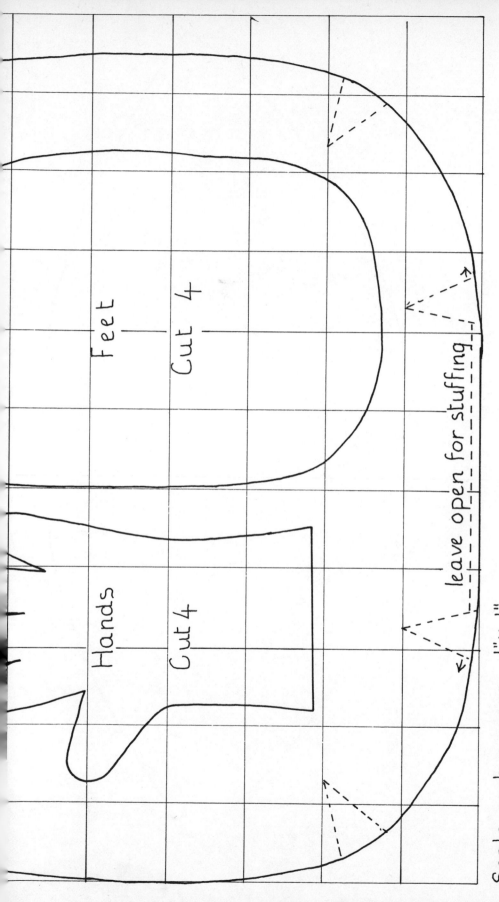

Feet

Cut 4

Hands

Cut 4

leave open for stuffing

Scale each square = 1" × 1"

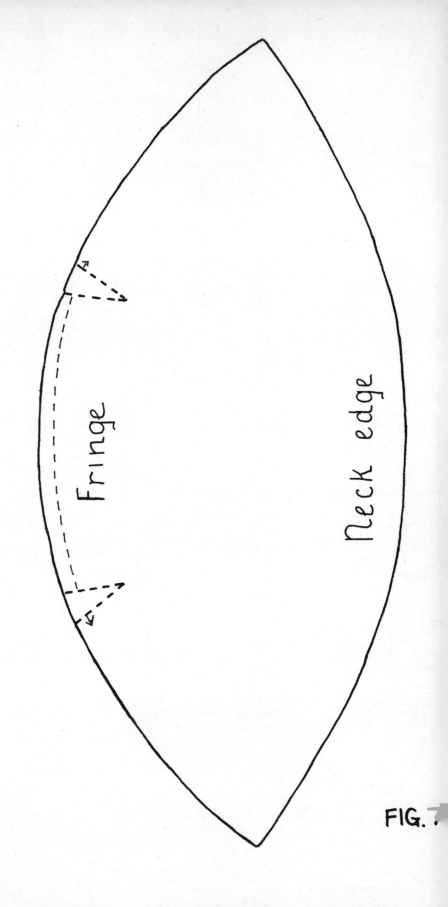

Fringe

Neck edge

34

FIG. 7

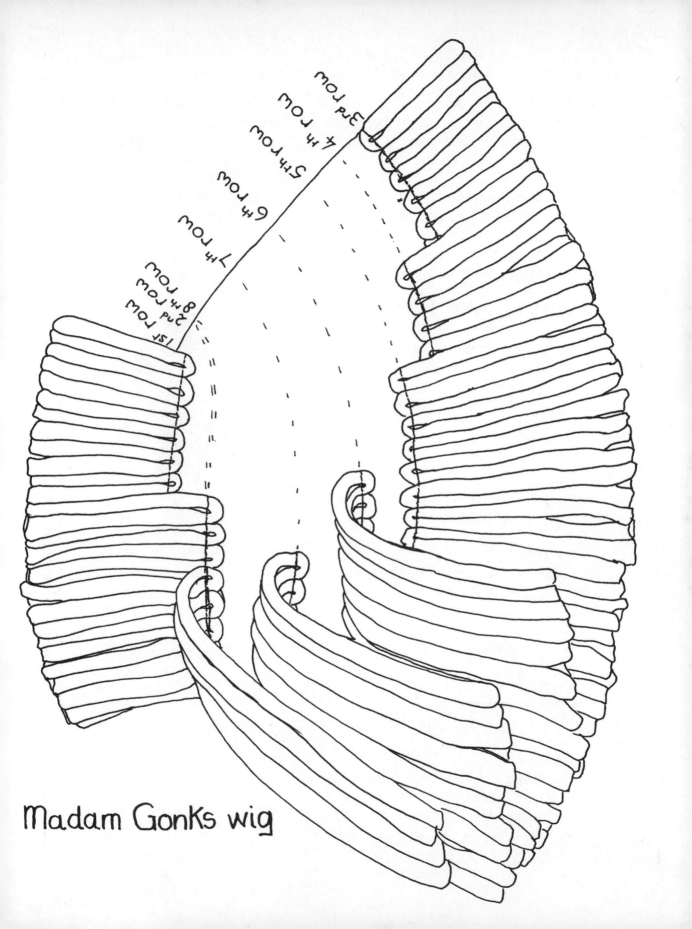

1st row
2nd row
8th row
7th row
6th row
5th row
4th row
3rd row

Madam Gonks wig

over this with two-inch card. Use two-and-a-half-inch card for third row and for the fourth use the three-inch card but, as you will see in Fig. 7, you bring the wool to the front of the wig as for the fringe and when you have stitched it, fold it back over the back wool. Fifth row the same. The sixth row is done in exactly the same way but is stitched on top of the second row of fringe and folded back. This not only gives a thick head of hair but covers the base completely so no line of stitching shows.

Arrange wig on Madam and stitch firmly. Cut wool loops carefully with sharp scissors and, if necessary, trim a little.

LION GLOVE PUPPET

For pattern (reduced scale) see facing page

MATERIALS

Piece of light brown woollen material about eleven inches by nineteen.

Piece of sateen the same size for lining.

About an ounce of double knitting in golden brown for mane and beard.

Small piece of tan felt for nose and eyes, and a piece of black felt for pupils.

Small amount of dark brown embroidery thread for outlining eyes, whiskers and mouth.

Threequarter-inch cardboard for winding wool.

METHOD

Cut lining a quarter of an inch smaller all round than outside of puppet or it will pucker when sewn into place.

Pencil or trace features on to puppet.

(*Above*) 1 Puppy, Baby Bunny, Cat and Ball (see Chapter 1)

(*Below*) 2 Octopus, Woolly Top and Leopard (see Chapter 2)

3 Baby Lamb, Madam Gonk and Lion Glove Puppet (see Chapter 3)

4 Baby Doll and Dark Lady Doll (see Chapter 4)

(*Left*) 5 Banana Man and Orange Lady (see Chapter 5)

(*Below*) 6 Llama and Little Wire People (see Chapter 6)

(*Left*) 7 Monkey (see Chapter 7)

(*Below*) 8 Dilly Duck, Dormouse, Cuddly Teddy and Squirrel (see Chapter 8)

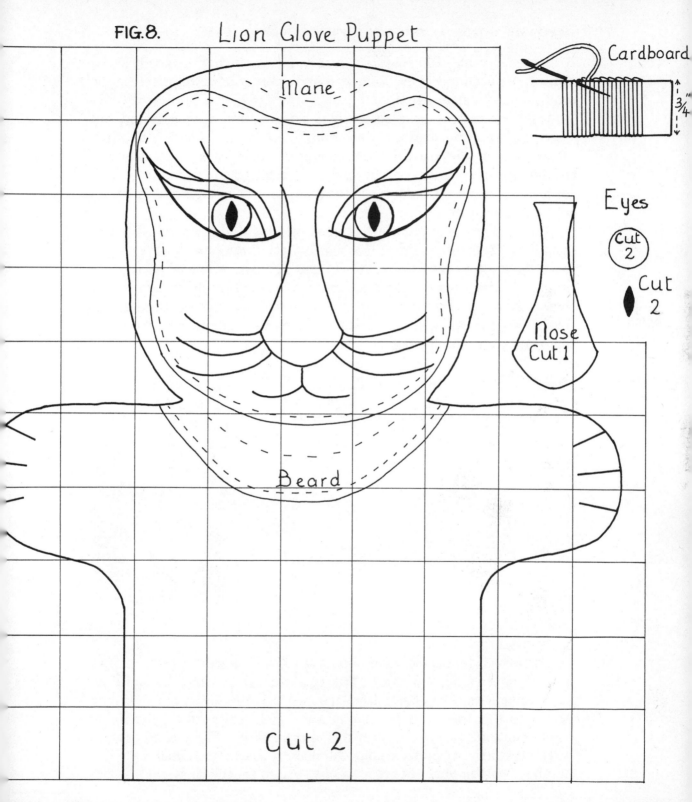

FIG.8. Lion Glove Puppet

Mane

Cardboard

¾"

Eyes

Cut 2

Cut 2

Nose Cut 1

Beard

Cut 2

ale each square = 1" x 1"

Sew eyes, pupils and nose on to face with tiny stitches then embroider. The upper outlining of eye is done in fine chain-stitch. All the rest of the embroidery in stem-stitch.

Make up puppet by placing right sides in and sewing round but leaving bottom open. Wind wool round card as in diagram and stitch along. Slip off cardboard and sew on puppet starting at front and working round face and beard as pattern. Then work round and round until back of head is covered. Do not make too many loops at a time or it becomes difficult to sew on firmly.

Make up lining and put into puppet, pushing well into paws. Turn in at wrist and slip-stitch lining into place. Make three claw marks on paws with the dark brown embroidery thread. The details for only one glove puppet is given but the same pattern can be used for other puppets. A black doll puppet can be made using the Dark Lady features as a guide and black wool for hair. Children find them great fun and many varieties can be made with a little imagination.

BABY LAMB

For pattern (to full scale) see pages 40–41

MATERIALS

Twenty-six by ten inches of almost any material with a rough surface, providing it is not too thick. The lamb in the picture was quite an achievement as it was made from the best part of a boy's old towelling shirt. As this was 'stretchy' it was lined with white calico, the lining being cut and sewn in one with the outer material. There is no need to stick to white; any pretty colour will make a charming animal.

About half an ounce of crêpe wool was used for the curly coat. It was made even more attractive as there is a silky thread running through the wool.

A small piece of black felt was used for the nose, eyebrows and pupils, and a piece of blue felt for the irises.

If the toy is intended for a very small child and so likely to spend a lot of time in the wash, it is better to make the nose of a washable material, either turning in the edges or buttonholing on to the lamb. The eyes and eyebrows can be embroidered.

Stuffing.

METHOD

Cut all pieces. Put both pieces of under-body together, right sides facing. Stitch about an inch and a half at either end. This leaves centre of under-body open for stuffing. Take one side of lamb and place right side against right side of inner legs and tack round one leg, underside of body and other leg. Stitch round. Repeat with the other side of lamb. Put upper part of lamb together and tack from where inner and outer legs are joined at front and right round upper part to back legs. It is important to tack carefully before stitching. Turn right side out.

The lamb needs stuffing firmly, particularly the legs, or it will not stand up. Stuff legs first, using small quantities of stuffing and pushing well down with the head of a knitting-needle. Now stuff the head, working the stuffing well in. Then stuff body and make sure it is firm before sewing up the under-body. Part of the success of this little creature is in the careful stuffing. Make ears and sew to head as shown in pattern.

Make the tail but do not stuff this too tightly or it may lose the curve. Sew on tail. Join nose at dotted lines as shown and sew into position. Make eyes and eyebrows.

Wind wool round pencil and oversew loops. Slide wool off pencil and begin sewing loops on just above one eyebrow over top of head and along back as shown in pattern. Second row from above other eyebrow. Make four rows of loops and sew right round body.

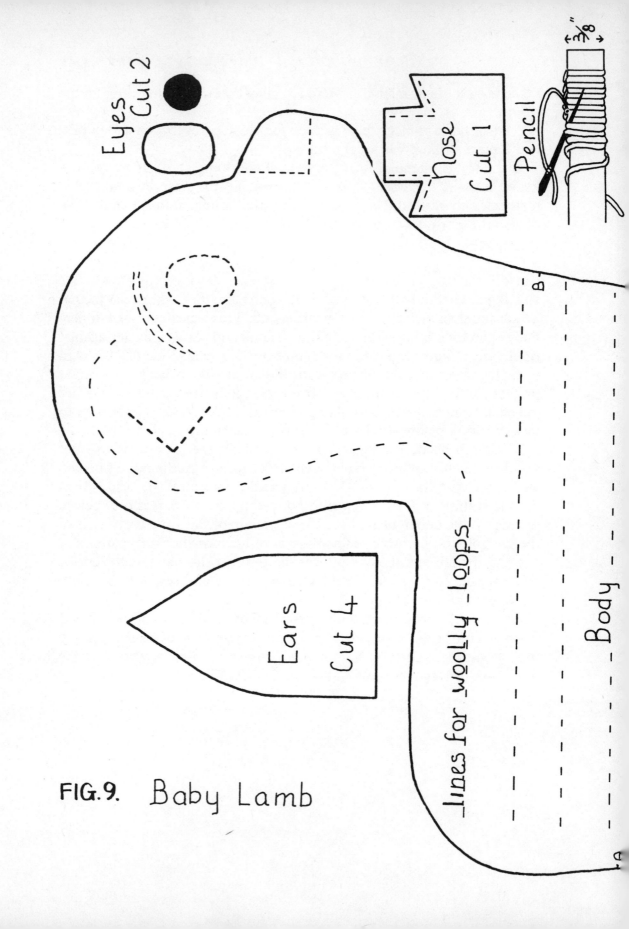

FIG. 9. Baby Lamb

Eyes
Cut 2

Nose
Cut 1

Pencil

3/8"

Ears
Cut 4

lines for woolly loops

Body

B

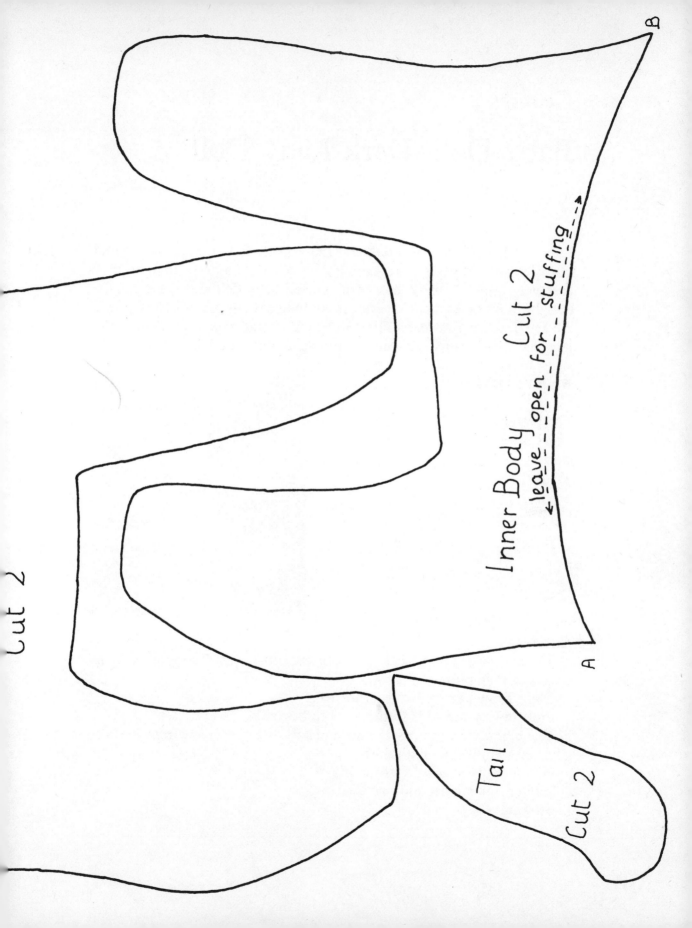

Cut 2

B

Inner Body   Cut 2
leave open for stuffing

A

Tail

Cut 2

Chapter 4

Baby Doll - Dark Lady Doll

Every young child loves a doll and those in the picture are simply and quickly made. What is more, even if new material has to be bought, they cost very little. A mask was used for the baby doll and these can be bought in many stores. However, if unobtainable in your district, please see the drawing provided. This can be either traced or copied on to the material with a fairly soft pencil. It is then embroidered.

BABY DOLL

For pattern (to full scale) see pages 46–47 and pattern for clothes (reduced scale) see pages 48–49

MATERIALS

Three-quarters of a yard of sateen curtain lining (the strongest) in cream or pale pink.

Light brown or golden wool for hair.

Embroidery thread if features are to be made.

The nightdress, bootees, bonnet and knickers were made from the best parts of a child's old nightdress.

Odd lengths of lace for trimming.

Ribbon for bonnet and bootees.

Stuffing.

METHOD

Body, arms and legs are cut in one. The head is darted to shape. Cut all parts carefully. Turnings have been allowed. Place right sides of body and limbs together and stitch about a quarter of an inch from edges, leaving neck and ankles open. Turn right side out and machine across body where marked on Fig. 10. This is to allow the doll to bend.

Cut two pieces for head and dart as in pattern. If the face is to be embroidered do that now. Use stem-stitch for the eyebrows in light brown. Two rows may be needed. Small pieces of felt may be used for mouth and eyes but embroidery will stand up to more wear and tear. Satin-stitch should be used. It is easier to start with the black for the pupil then work round it with blue for the iris and finish with a little white for the edges. The mouth is simple to work in satin-stitch.

If a mask is to be used this should be sewn on when the doll is complete but before the hair is made.

Having sewn the darts in the head, place right sides of head together and stitch round. Turn right side out.

Sew back and front of upper part of feet, stitch on sole and turn right side out.

Stuff upper part of body, pushing stuffing well down into the arms first and then filling the body right to neck edge. Now stuff head very firmly right to neck. Turn edge in and oversew to body. It is important to stuff neck very firmly. Stuff lower part of body right to ankles. Stuff feet and then push ankles into top of feet.and oversew firmly. Hair is made by winding wool round and round a pencil. When pencil is covered oversew the loops right along to hold and then slide off pencil. Arrange hair round face and stitch firmly. The bonnet can then be sewn on or the head can be covered with rows of the looped wool and the bonnet just tied on.

CLOTHES

Knickers. Seam legs and then join front and back seams. Trim legs with narrow lace. Make narrow hem at waist for elastic.

Nightdress. Join shoulder and side seams. Cut opening at back for about four inches. Hem each side of opening and then fold over and stitch to form placket. Gather a narrow piece of lace and the neck edge together to fit doll's neck. Fold lace downwards and then bind with a piece of bias binding or an inch-wide piece of the material. It is easier if you

43

cut this on the bias. Fasten with press stud. Trim wrist edges with lace and run shirring elastic round edge of material to gather. Hem bottom.

Bonnet. Hem bottom then make a tiny edge all round curved edge and gather to fit face. Trim with lace and ribbons to tie.

Bootees. Seam all round. Trim tops with lace. Sew a piece of ribbon at the back of each bootee to tie round ankle.

DARK LADY

For pattern (to full scale) see pages 46–47 and pattern for clothes (reduced scale) see pages 48–49

This is made in exactly the same way as the baby doll but using dark brown or black sateen. The feet were made with a small piece of bright red material to form shoes. The mouth is wider and can be made even wider if you wish. The hair is made of black crêpe wool but any coarse black wool may be used.

To make the hair. Cut a piece of cardboard about three and a half to four inches wide and about five inches long. Wind the wool evenly round it and then oversew at one side. Slip it off the cardboard without cutting and sew to doll's head from centre front to back. Sew underpart to head to hold in place but leaving top loops free. If preferred the wool can be wound round a pencil in the same way as baby doll or it can be wound on a piece of cardboard about an inch wide and after oversewing, cut one edge. In each of these cases the wool must be sewn all over the head of the doll.

Once you have the basic idea for these dolls you can make endless variations.

44

CLOTHES FOR DARK LADY

A strip of material one and a half inches wide and sixteen inches long for band. A piece of gay material thirty-eight inches by nine inches for skirt. Small piece of any soft white material for blouse and knickers.

Skirt. Join back of skirt leaving an opening of two and a half inches. Hem each side of opening and then fold over and stitch to make placket. Gather waist to fit doll and insert into band. Place centre of band to centre front of skirt, right sides facing. Stitch right along skirt. Turn band over and hem right along band and to inside of skirt. The long ends are then used to tie skirt.

The knickers are cut long enough to reach ankles. Sew leg seams and then join front and back seam. Hem for waist elastic. Finish ankles with a straight edge of narrow lace.

Blouse. Stitch side and shoulder seams. Gather neck into band after hemming opening at back. Press stud for fastening. Gather wrists with shirring elastic. No lace was used for blouse. A necklace is a MUST for this gay little doll. Any beads may be used. Small, brass curtain-rings may be sewn just under short hair for ear-rings.

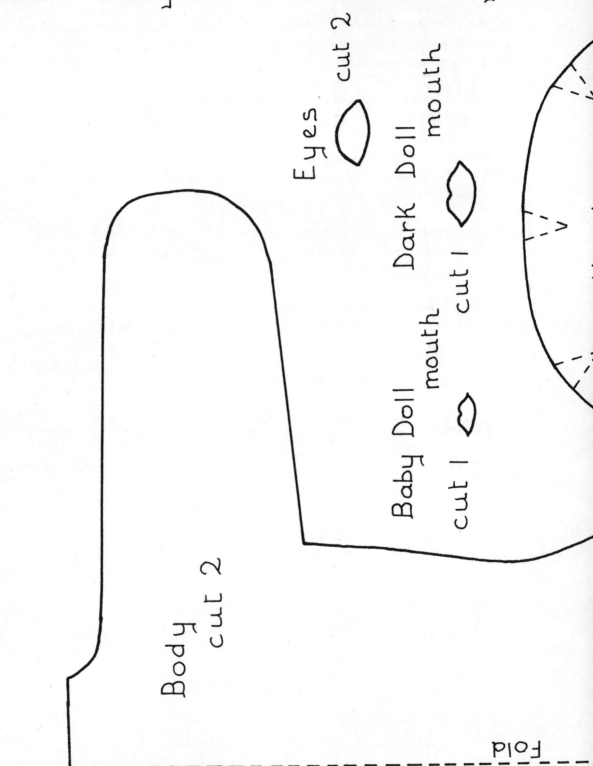

FIG. 10. Baby Doll and Dark Lady Doll

Eyes
cut 2

Dark Doll
mouth
cut 1

Baby Doll
mouth
cut 1

Body
cut 2

Fold

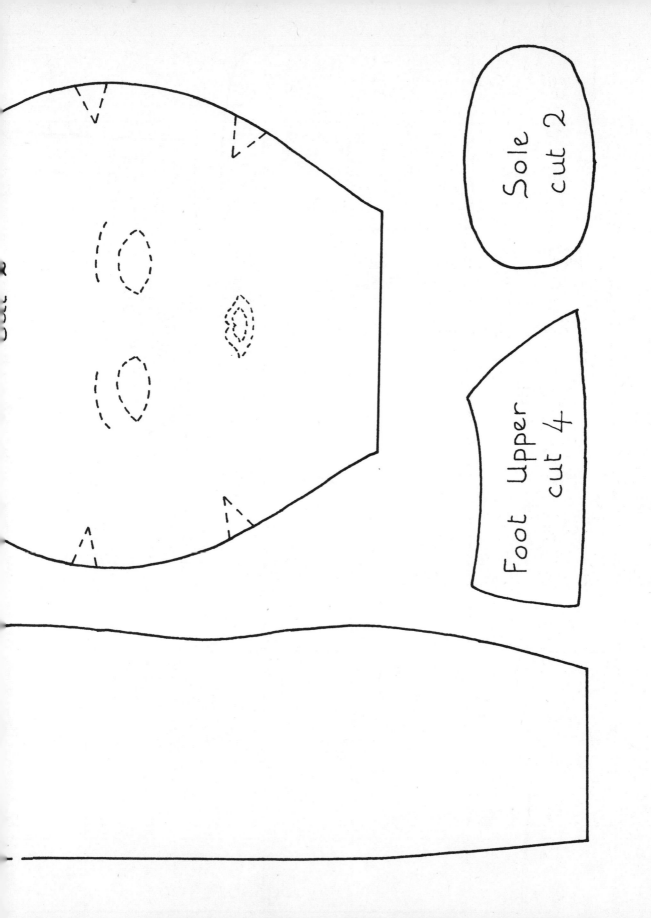

Sole
cut 2

Foot Upper
cut 4

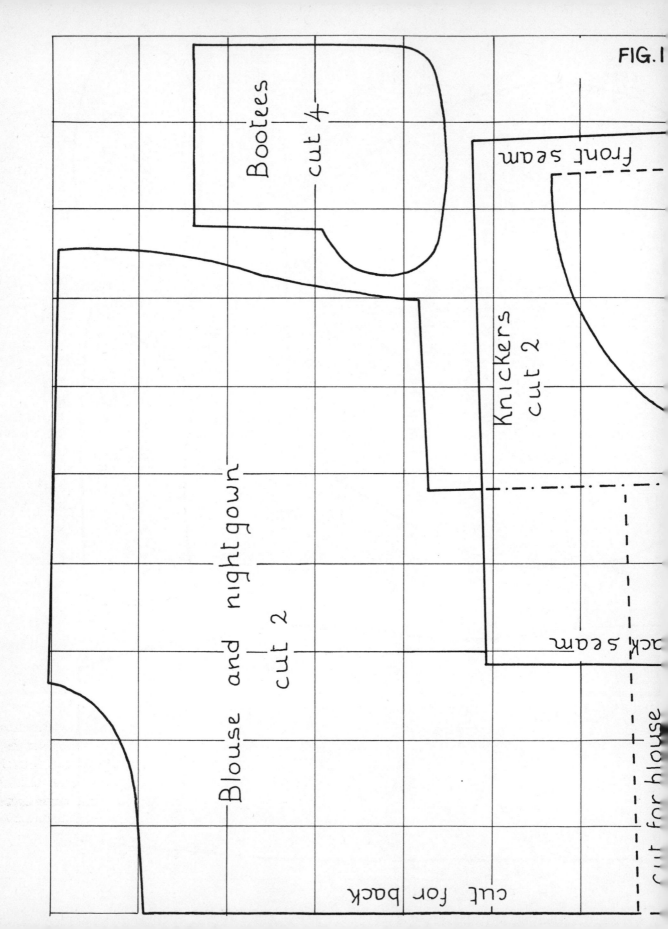

FIG.1

Bootees
cut 4

Front seam

Knickers
cut 2

Blouse and nightgown
cut 2

back seam

cut for back

cut for blouse

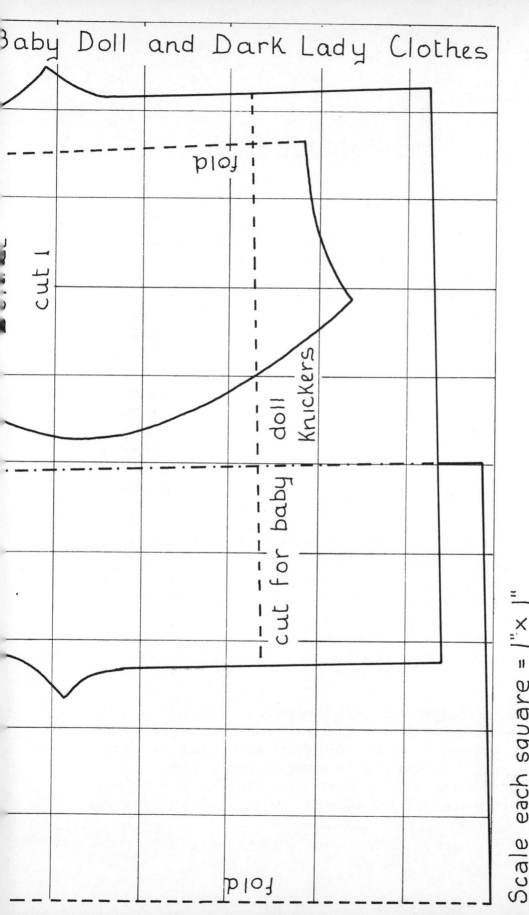

Baby Doll and Dark Lady Clothes

cut 1

fold

doll Knickers

cut for baby

fold

fold

Scale each square = 1"x 1"

Chapter 5

Banana Man - Orange Lady

These can be made with any firm material that does not fray easily. Bonded nylon was used for the examples but they can be made in felt.

BANANA MAN

For pattern (to full scale) see pages 52–53

MATERIALS

A piece of bonded nylon in bright yellow ten inches by twelve.

Small piece of brown felt for top of head, arms, legs and stalk.

A piece of white felt for hat and tiny pieces in red and white for features.

A small amount of embroidery thread for outlining eyebrows and lashes and a small length of natural for nose.

Fifteen inches of wire for arms and legs.

Small amount of stuffing.

METHOD

Cut all pieces and make features on front piece. Mouth can be made with small piece of felt and sewn on or embroidered. Stitch body pieces together on wrong side, first marking where arms are to go as this must be left open for inserting wire. Leave top and bottom open.

Stitch round arms and legs close to edges. Cut wire in half and bend ends into tiny loops so that it will not pierce felt. Bind wire tightly with

50

strips of nylon and sew tightly to loops at ends. Push wire right through openings at sides. Pull felt arms over wire and sew into position. Cut places for legs as shown in pattern. Bend leg wire as for arms and bind. Push through cuts and pull felt legs over and sew as for arms.

Stuff banana firmly from both ends.

Join stalk as dotted line in pattern. Push bottom of banana in stalk and stitch. Tuck in edges at top and sew on square of brown felt.

Sew band of hat into circle then oversew top to band. Oversew brim to band. Stitch to head at jaunty angle.

ORANGE LADY

For pattern (to full scale) see page 54

MATERIALS

Bright orange-bonded nylon was used. Felt could be substituted but nylon looks better.

Small pieces of cream felt for arms and legs. Bonded nylon can be used but it must be stitched on the wrong side and turned right side out which is tricky as arms and legs are so small.

Black crêpe wool for fringe and hair.

A hairpin and some gold thread for comb.

A piece of black lace for mantilla.

Stuffing.

METHOD

Cut all pieces and make features. Sew pieces together leaving opening at back for stuffing. Make holes for arms and legs as shown. Cut wire in half and proceed as for banana man. Wind wool round a piece of half-inch cardboard for fringe, oversew along one side and slip off card. Stitch in position and trim. Sew wool round and round on head and then make a bun on top as diagram. Bend hairpin as in Fig. 13 and bind with gold or silver thread. Push into head either side of bun and sew into position. Arrange black lace over this and sew.

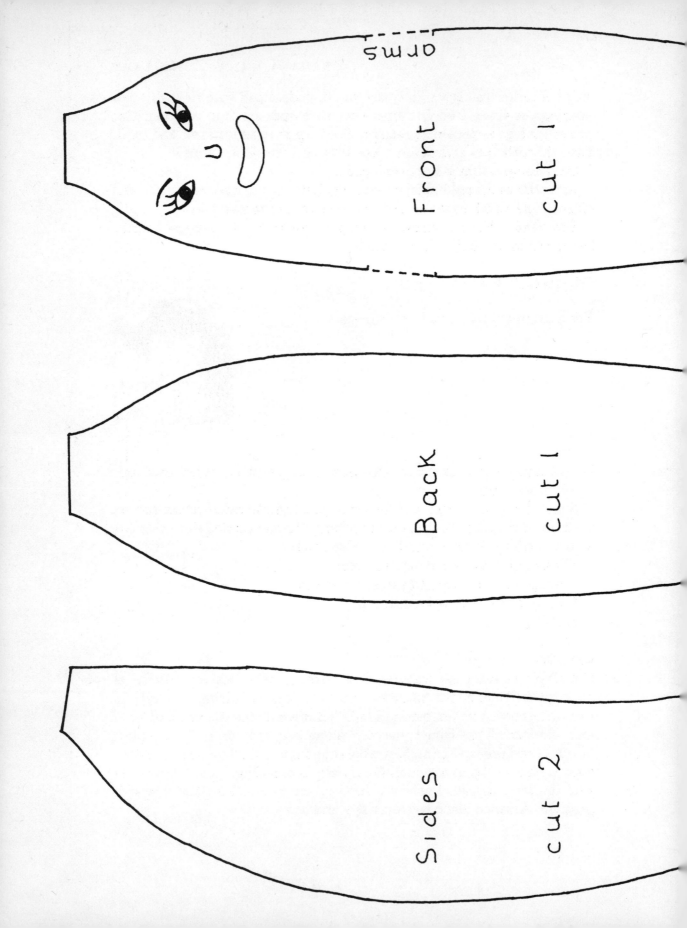

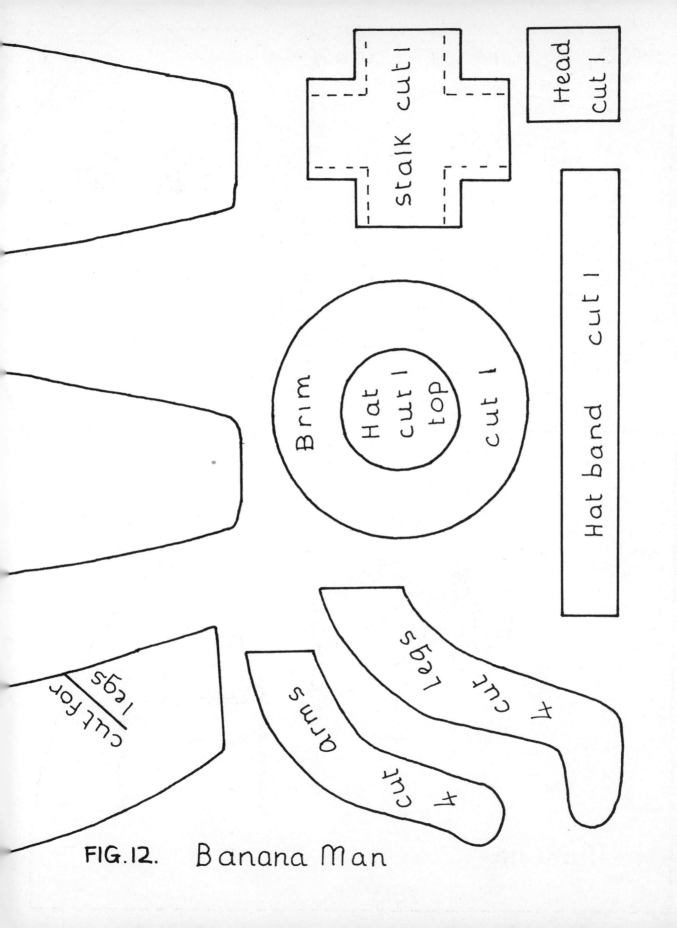

FIG.12. Banana Man

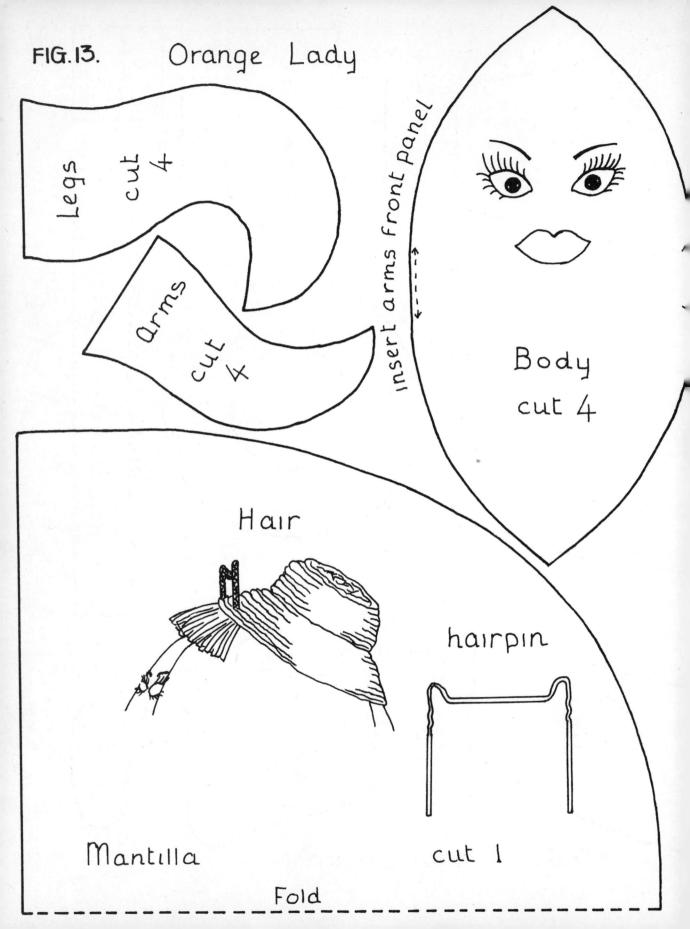

FIG. 13.   Orange Lady

Legs cut 4

Arms cut 4

insert arms front panel

Body cut 4

Hair

hairpin

Mantilla

cut 1

Fold

Chapter 6

Little Wire People-Llama

LITTLE WIRE PEOPLE

For pattern (to full scale) see
pages 56–57

Once you have mastered the basic principles, these wire toys can be made
any size. They cost very little as odds and ends of material can be used.

MATERIALS

Wire for base. Wire which is used to bind round crates is ideal and the
local hardware store is usually only to glad to get rid of it! It is firm
but not too tough and bends easily.

Small pieces of material for body and head and a little stuffing.

Strips of nylon for padding limbs and body and narrow tape for final
binding. The type used for binding lampshade frames is the best.

Small piece of flesh-coloured material for head and hands.

Fine wool for hair.

Material for clothes. Felt was used for those in Plate 6 but any material
can be used.

Features can either be embroidered or pencilled in with nylon-tipped
pens. There are plenty of coloured ones on the market with fine tips
which are good for this.

METHOD

Cut a piece of wire about seventeen inches long and bend in half, rounding the top as diagram, then making a twist to form neck. Cut another piece about nine inches long, make a small loop at either end and insert under twist of neck. Now make another twist to hold arm wire in position and then fold arms right over and bind join. A stitch or two will hold binding in place, or a spot of quick-drying glue can be used. Loop ends of legs and bend to form feet.

Cut circle of material about four inches in diameter and run a draw thread round edge and gather, leaving enough opening for stuffing. Stuff firmly then draw thread tight and fasten off. Push this ball under loop of wire which forms head and stitch to wire, gathered end to neck. Cut two ovals of the flesh-coloured material, each slightly larger than head. Cover face with one and stitch into position. Place the other piece at back of head, turn in edge and slip-stitch to front piece. This join will be covered by the hair.

Cut a piece of material about four inches long and one and a half to two inches wide. Fold over and stitch sides to make bag. Stuff and sew up. Stitch to body wire. Bind limbs with strips of nylon for padding – only a little round hands and feet or they will be too big. Stitch or glue ends. Make tiny bags of flesh-coloured material and pull over hands and stitch.

FIG. 14.

Little Wire People

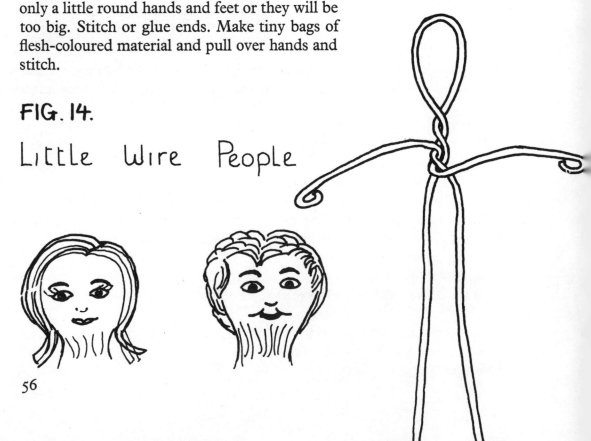

56

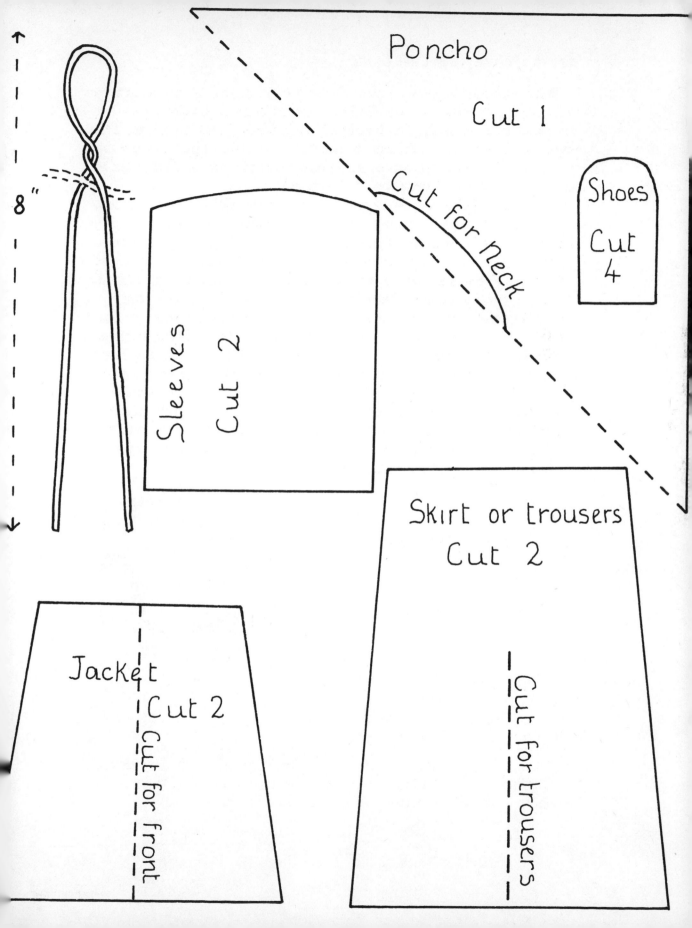

Poncho

Cut 1

Cut for Neck

Shoes
Cut
4

8"

Sleeves
Cut 2

Skirt or trousers
Cut 2

Cut for trousers

Jacket
Cut 2

Cut for front

Bind with narrow tape, starting at the neck and then down one arm to wrist and then back to body. One turn round body then down the other arm and back to body. Bind carefully round body and then legs. The tape can then be stitched firmly to the under-binding. The shoes are cut from tiny pieces of felt, tacked into position on the feet and trimmed to size and then sewn firmly round the edges.

The features should now be marked either with embroidery or pencil. The hair is made by winding wool on cardboard. It can be made any length you wish, oversewn along one side after winding and then sewn to the head. It is fun to experiment with this. It can be short or long, loose or plaited. Curly hair can be made by winding wool round a pencil and, after oversewing along one side, sewn on to the head without cutting.

Making the clothes out of felt is very simple and are more or less 'moulded' on to the dolls. Ideas are given on the pattern and can be made either larger or smaller as they are very simple. They can be decorated with braid, narrow fringe or embroidery. The sleeveless jacket is just two pieces sewn at shoulders and sides, leaving an opening for the arms and then cut up centre front. Sleeves are made with a scrap of light material sewn on to the doll before the jacket. Lace sleeves are very attractive.

These dolls make good models for period costume dressing. Tiny ones can be made for a doll's house family.

LLAMA

For pattern (to full scale) see pages 60–61

MATERIALS

A piece of material in cream or natural twenty-four inches by eleven.

One ounce of nylon knitting in cream or natural for coat. Wool is not suitable as it will not brush into a really silky finish.

Two pieces of wire each nine and a half inches for legs and an eight-and-a-half-inch piece for head and neck.

Strips of nylon for binding.

Small pieces of felt for features.

Needleful of golden-brown embroidery thread for mouth.

Two pieces of cardboard, one four and a half inches deep and about six inches long, the other two and a half inches deep by six inches.

Stuffing.

METHOD

Cut all pieces. With right sides facing, stitch round body from A to B (Fig. 15). Join inner body to outer leaving underside open for stuffing. Turn right side out.

Loop wire for head and bind, then push into head. Stuff head and neck, very small pieces at a time, using the head of a small knitting-needle. Bend wire for front legs making small loops at ends. Bind well so that no further stuffing is necessary for legs once wire is in position. Loop neck wire on to front leg wire. Bind and bend wire for hind-legs and insert. Stuff body very firmly and oversew.

Sew features into position as pattern. The eyelids are edged with black buttonhole-stitching to form eyelashes and then sewn on with invisible nylon thread. Make ears and tail and sew into position. To make mane and undercoat wind nylon round two-and-a-half-inch card. Wind evenly and without stretching. Oversew one side before cutting. Sew into position as pattern. The top coat is made in two pieces on the four-and-a-half-inch card. Wind the first side and oversew before cutting. Open out and stitch right along the oversewing for extra strength. Fold back and sew right along centre back with the coat on the opposite side from which you want it to fall. When you have sewn right along, fold it back and then do the same with the other side. This prevents a gap at centre coat. Trim mane and brush round neck. Brush coat gently to form soft hair and trim if necessary.

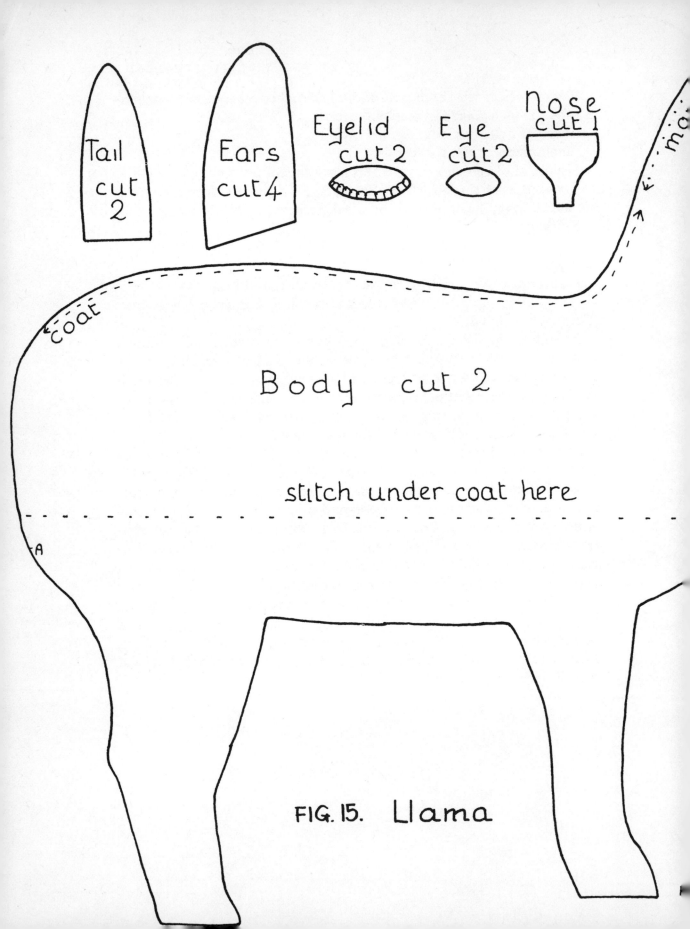

Tail cut 2

Ears cut 4

Eyelid cut 2

Eye cut 2

Nose cut 1

mo...

coat

Body cut 2

stitch under coat here

A

FIG. 15. Llama

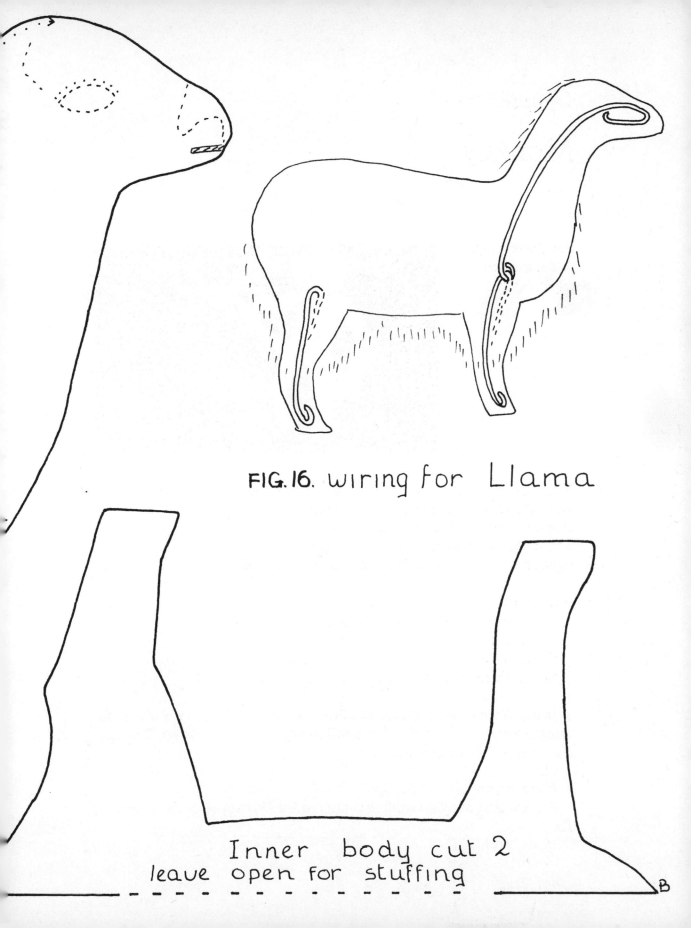

FIG. 16. wiring for Llama

Inner body cut 2
leave open for stuffing

B

Chapter 7

Monkey

For patterns (to
full scale) see
pages 64–70

This toy – twenty-nine inches high – is rather complicated but not
beyond any reasonably good needlewoman. The end result is so charming
that it is well worth the time and trouble. The monkey in the photograph
was made in white fur cloth with pink felt face and pink velour for ears,
hands and feet. It would look equally well in brown.

MATERIALS

Half a yard of forty-eight-inch wide fur cloth.
Felt for face twelve inches by twelve.
Eighth of a yard of velour for ears, hands and feet.
Small pieces of brown and black felt for eyes.

Wire: Twenty-four inches for head and body. Forty-two inches for
arms. Twenty-seven inches for legs. Twenty-four inches for tail. Twenty-
eight inches for fingers and toes.
Pliers.
Eight inches of cord for lips.
A great deal of nylon stuffing is needed for this toy as it must be very

firmly stuffed. You will also need a lot of nylon strips for binding the wire.

Fur cloth must be cut so that pile brushes downwards.

METHOD

Cut out all pieces. Sew darts in front and back of head and join front and back together. Tuck fur under round hole for face and tack. Join large and small darts at side of face and make small darts at side of nose. Fit into cut-out piece of head and sew into position.

Join shoulders. Join side seams of body, leaving open from shoulder to mark X on pattern for arms. Make small dart at crotch. Sew seams of arms and legs. Join body and head together. Make circle for head in body wire as Fig. 19. Wind arm wire round body wire at shoulder height. Bend ends of arm wire into small loops and bind well as this forms the middle fingers. Bind all wire with plenty of nylon strips particularly at joins. Fit wire through body up into head, easing arm wire through armholes. Stuff head firmly using the head of a long knitting-needle. Fit arms over wire and sew into place. Stuff body leaving space at bottom in order to be able to bend body wire round leg wire.

Stuff arms from wrist end. This was done with a long screwdriver as the arms are narrow and it is necessary to make sure the padding is evenly and firmly placed all round the wire.

Sew feet and hands on wrong side and turn right side out. It is rather difficult to push the fingers and toes out and the head of a small knitting-needle was used for this.

Cut wire to fit fingers, bending the wire into small loops at ends as diagram and binding so that no extra stuffing is needed. Push wire into thumb and first finger and then into third and fourth. Slip arm wire through thumb and first finger wire and into middle finger. Stuff all round hand wire. Tuck edge of fur cloth under at wrist. Push hand under cloth and sew into position. Same with other hand.

Loop ends of leg wire and bind for middle toe then bind rest of wire. Fit leg wire through leg holes. Bend body wire over leg wire, binding join, and finish stuffing body. Draw legs over wire and sew into position. Stuff legs as for arms. Continue with feet as for hands.

No pattern is given for tail as this is just two strips of material twenty-two inches long, two and a half inches wide at body tapering to half an inch at end. Stitch on wrong side and turn right side out. Bend tail wire at tip into a small loop and bind tightly with strips of nylon, sewing

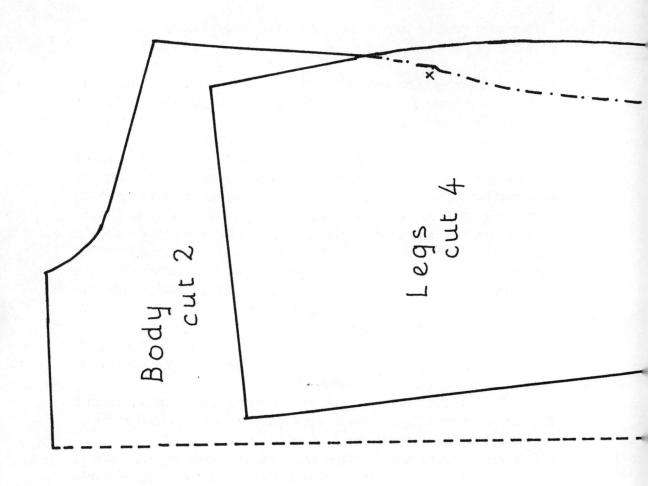

Body
cut 2

Legs
cut 4

FIG. 17a.   Monkey 1
[see also 17b. overleaf]

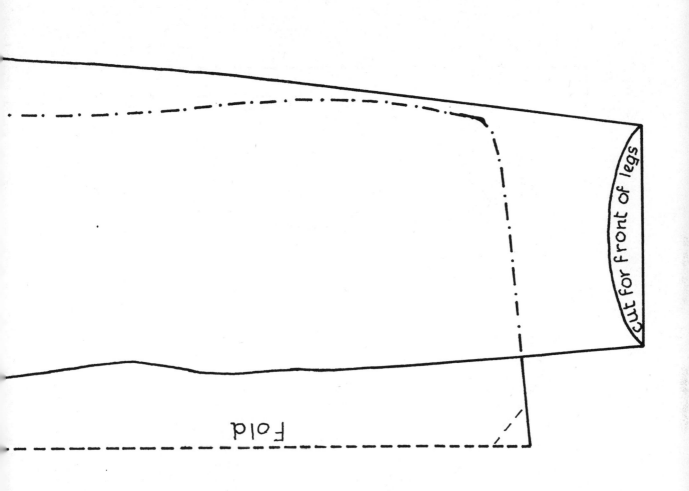

Cut for front of legs

Fold

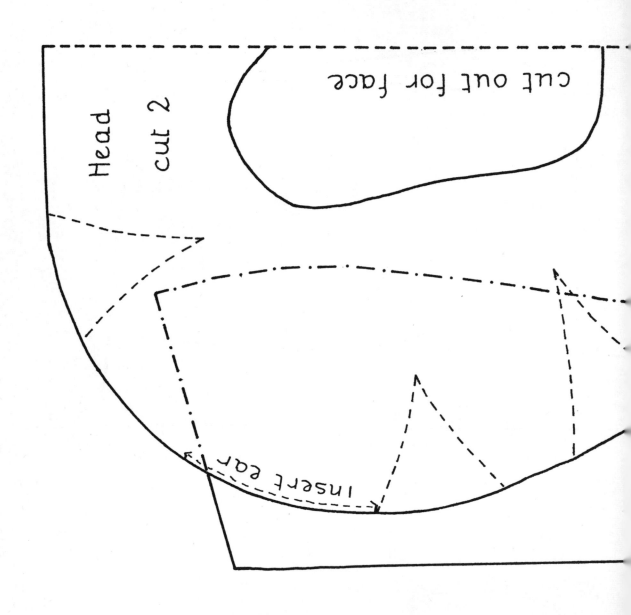

Head

cut 2

cut out for face

insert ear

FIG. 17b. Monkey 1

Eyebrows

cut 2

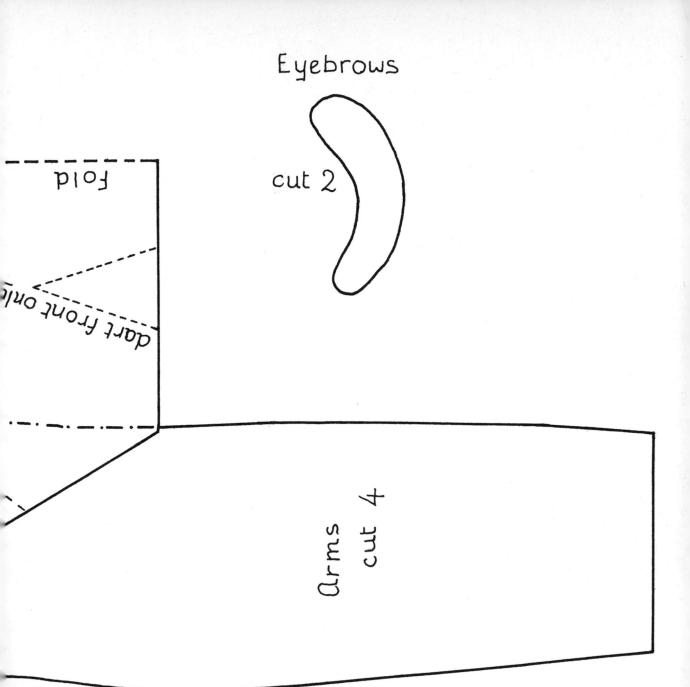

fold

dart front only

Arms

cut 4

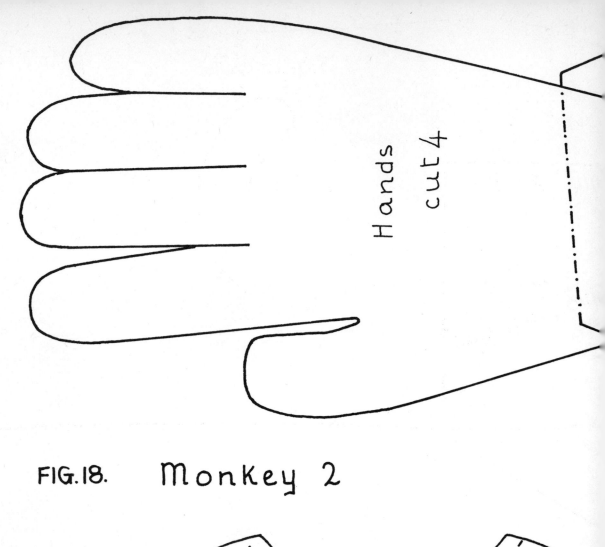

Hands
cut 4

FIG.18.   Monkey 2

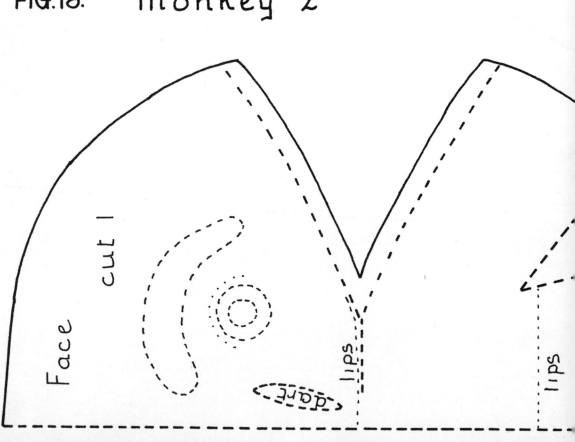

Face   cut 1

dart

lips

lips

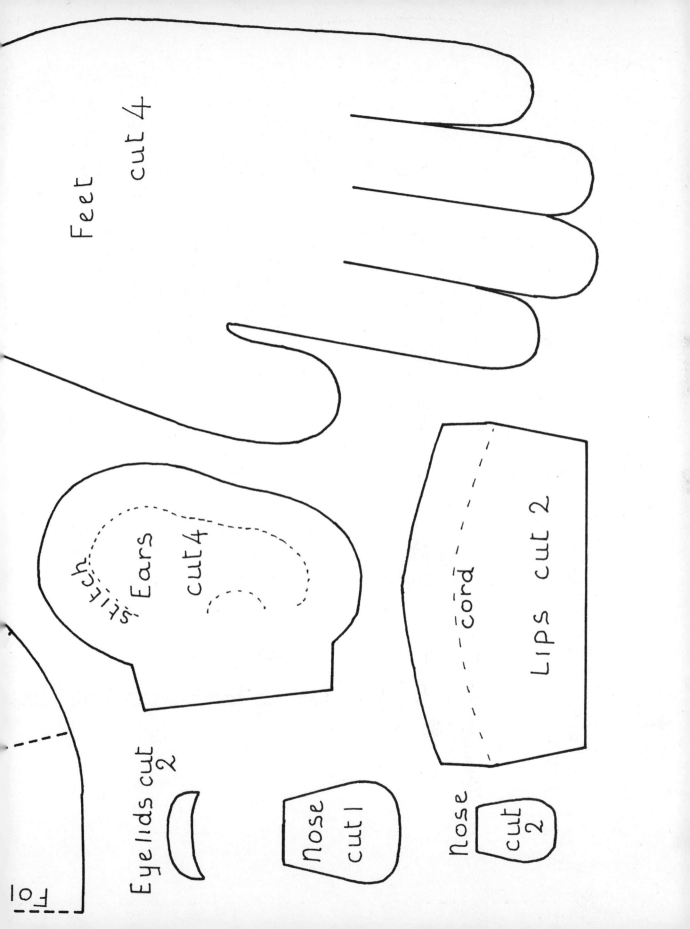

Feet
cut 4

stitch
Ears
cut 4

cord
Lips cut 2

Eyelids cut
2

Nose
cut 1

nose
cut
2

Fol

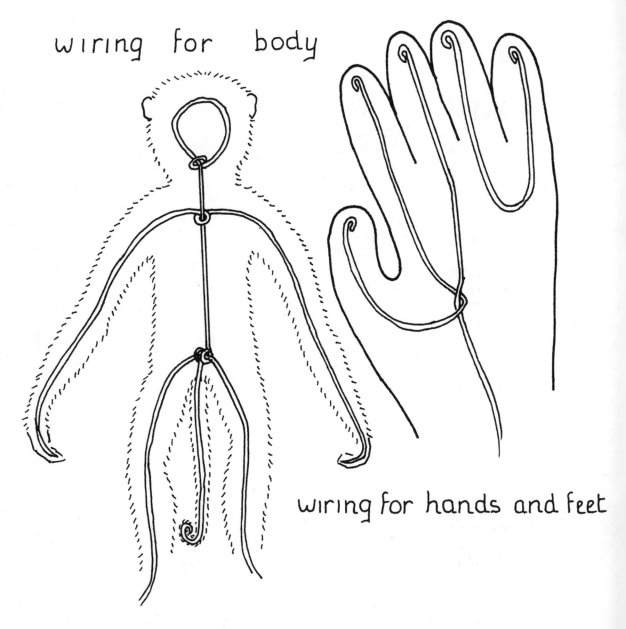

FIG. 19. Monkey-Wiring

wiring for body

wiring for hands and feet

firmly at loop. Draw tail over wire and stuff firmly. Make a half-inch hole at back of body about an inch above crotch. Bend end of tail wire, push into hole and hook over leg wire. Insert pliers into hole and pinch wire firmly into position. Add more stuffing through hole and at top of tail before sewing into position.

Make ears up on wrong side and turn right side out. Pad very slightly. Stitch round as pattern. Open seams on head at ear marks. Insert ears in position, flattening back and stitching carefully.

TO MAKE FEATURES

Turn edges of fur cloth for eyebrows under and sew in position. Sew brown eyes and black pupils into place. Sew eyelids on as dotted line. They will then stand away from eyes. Place padding under nose and sew into position. Turn lips over at curve, inserting cord as you sew. Sew upper lip into position as pattern, leaving a little fullness so that lip protrudes slightly. Sew lower lip, slightly overlapping upper lip.

Chapter 8

Knitted Toys:
Dormouse-Cuddly Teddy-Dilly Duck-Squirrel

Knitted toys are simple to make once you have mastered the basic principles. The knitting must be firm and close or the stuffing will show through. Cheaper wools are often better for toys as it is rougher in texture and stands up to hard wear. They take very little wool and often can be made with left-overs from garments. Many wool shops sell odd balls of wool cheaply and I usually pounce on these, whatever the colour, knowing they will come in useful at one time or another.

All toys given (see Plate 8) were knitted in stocking-stitch throughout – one row plain, one row purl, except duck's wings for which g-st. was used. The dormouse, squirrel and duck were knitted in stocking-stitch but knitted into the back of the stitches on the plain row. This is not only firm but gives a 'woven' appearance. The teddy was knitted in ordinary stocking-stitch because the wool was not only coarse but had a silky thread running through it and the needles were fine for the thickness of the wool.

When knitting small pieces such as arms, legs or ears it is quicker to use two balls of wool and knit two together at the same time. Cast on one piece with the first ball and then cast on the other on the same needle with the second ball. If you have not done this before it is worth trying as it avoids the business of carefully measuring the second piece by the first.

Tension has not been given as, so long as the size of needles and the thickness of wool stated are used, the size will vary very little. The knitting should move along the needles smoothly, neither tight nor loose. All casting on was done in the usual way on two needles, unless otherwise stated.

To cast off with a rounded edge knit the first two stitches together, cast off in the usual way to the last two stitches, knit these together before passing the last loop over.

Increasing is usually done by knitting into the front and back of a stitch but in some cases it is done by picking up the loop between two stitches. When this method is used it is clearly stated.

ABBREVIATIONS

alt. = alternate
beg. = beginning
dec. = decrease(ing)
g-st. = garter stitch (all rows knit)
inc. = increase(ing)
ins. = inches
K. = knit
P. = purl
patt. = pattern

p.s.s.o. = pass slipped stitch over
sl. = slip
st. = stitch
sts. = stitches
st-st. = stocking-stitch (1 row knit
      1 row purl)
t.b.l. = through back of loops
tog. = together

DORMOUSE

MATERIALS

This toy, just four inches high, takes less than an ounce of 4-ply wool and was knitted in golden brown.

A small length of 2-ply wool in dark brown was used for eyes and nose.

A pair of No. 12 knitting-needles.

Wool needle.

Small amounts of stuffing.

Body and head are knitted in one piece. St-st. throughout, knitting into back of stitches on plain rows.

METHOD

Body and head

Cast on 56 sts.

Starting with a plain row knit 6 rows.

7th row. K.6. K.2 tog. t.b.l. Rep. to end of row.

Next row. P.

Next row. K.5. K.2 tog. t.b.l. Rep. to end of row.

Next row. P.

Next row. K.4. K.2 tog. t.b.l. Rep. to end of row. (35 sts.)

K.1¾ ins. without shaping end with a purl row.

Next row. K.3. K.2 tog. t.b.l. Rep. to end of row.

Continue decreasing in same way until 14 sts. remain. The last row will be K.1. K.2 tog. t.b.l. until end of row.

Next row. P.

Leaving about twelve inches of wool break off and thread on wool needle. Thread needle through loops of sts. and draw up tightly. Fasten firmly but do not break off wool. This forms top of head. Now sew back seam and fasten off.

Ears

Cast on 8 sts. K.4 rows st-st.

5th row. K.3. K.2 tog. t.b.l. K.3.

Next row. P.

Next row. K.2. Sl.1. K.2 tog. p.s.s.o. K.2.

Next row P.

Next row. K.1. Sl.1. K.2 tog. p.s.s.o. K.1.

Break off short length of wool and thread on needle. Thread through remaining 3 sts. and draw up. Now run thread round edge of ear and gather slightly so that the ear has a curve. Fasten off. Make two.

Arms

Cast on 10 sts. K.1½ ins. Break off wool leaving a few ins. Thread on needle and draw through the stitches. Sew seam.

Feet

Cast on 10 sts. K. 1 in. and fasten off as for arms.

TO MAKE UP

Stuff body and sew up bottom with flat seam. Thread the needle with a short length of wool and (as invisibly as possible) make a gathering thread about an inch and a half from top of head. Gather very slightly and fasten off. This forms neck. Sew on ears about half an inch apart and slightly to back of head.

Stuff arms. Sew up shoulder ends flat and sew to body. The feet are flattened and sewn to base without stuffing.

The features are very simple. With the dark brown wool make two stitches for each eye about half an inch from the top of the head and each stitch just over a quarter of an inch long. The nose is made with four stitches. To do this draw the wool through the knitting at the point for the first eye and make a tiny stitch holding the end of the wool firmly so that it doesn't slip right through. Now make the two stitches for the eye and then pass the wool through to the other eye and make the eye stitches. Pass the wool through to the nose and make four stitches. Fasten off by taking the wool under the nose and back before cutting off. Cut off the end of wool where you started.

CUDDLY TEDDY

This toy (fourteen inches) is particularly suitable for a child from seven or eight months onwards, as it is easily grasped by arms or legs and there is nothing that can injure a baby and nothing about Teddy that can be injured! Plain stocking-stitch throughout.

MATERIALS

Three ounces of rather coarse double knitting.
A yard or so of 2-ply dark brown for features and claws.
A short length of white to mark sides of eyes.
Pair of No. 11 needles.
Ribbon for neck.

METHOD
Front legs and body
Using two balls of wool cast on 10 sts. twice.
 1st row. K.
 2nd row. P.
 Next row. Inc. in 1st st. K. to last st. inc.
 Next row. P.

Continue inc. on each K. row until 16 sts. P.1 row.

Next row. K.6. K.2 tog. t.b.l. K.2 tog. K.6.

Next row. P.

Next row. K.6 inc. in next 2 sts. K.6.

K.3 ins. ending with a P. row.

K. right across both legs breaking off second ball of wool and fasten securely by weaving in and out of back of sts. (32 sts.)

K. $2\frac{1}{2}$ ins. ending with a P. row.

Dec. at beginning and end of next row.

K.5 rows.

Inc. at beginning and end of next row.

K. until work measures 4 ins. from crotch, ending with a purl row.

K.2 tog. at beginning and end of each knit row until 26 sts.

Continue without decreasing until work measures $6\frac{1}{2}$ ins. from crotch.

Cast off 5 sts. at beginning of next 2 rows. (16 sts.)

K.4 rows without shaping. Cast off.

Back legs and body

Cast on 16 sts. for each leg. K. until legs measured same as front legs from where 16 sts. were formed. Now continue as for front.

Arms

With two balls of wool cast on 24 sts. twice. Inc. at each end of every K. row until 30 sts.

K.3 rows.

Dec. at beginning and end of next and every following 4th row until 22 sts.

K.9 rows.

Next row. K.2 tog. * K.3. K.2 tog. Rep. from * to end of row. (17 sts.)

K.3 rows.

Next row. Inc. in 1st st. K.7. Inc. in next st. K. to last st. inc. (20 sts.)

Next row. K.2 tog. all along row. Break off wool leaving about 12 ins. Thread wool on wool needle and pass through loops. Sew these loops flat, 5 sts. either side. Fasten securely and sew seam.

Head (3 pieces)

(1) Left cheek:

Cast on 12 sts.

K.6 rows.

Next row. Inc. in 1st st. K. to last st. Inc.
Next row. P.
Next row. Inc. in 1st st. * K.2. Inc. in next st. Rep. from * to end of row. (22 sts.)
Next row. P. **
Next row. K. to last st. inc.
Next row. P.
Next row. Inc. in 1st st. K. to end.
Three rows without shaping.
Next row. K.2 tog. K. to end of row.
Next row. Cast off 5. P. to end of row.
Two rows without shaping. ***
Next row. K.2 tog. at beginning and end of row. (17 sts.)
Three rows without shaping.
K.2 tog. at beginning and end of every K. row until 9 sts. remain.
Cast off, rounding edge by knitting 2 tog. at beg. and end.

(2) Right cheek:
Cast on 12 and continue as left cheek until **
Next row. Inc. in 1st st. K. to end.
Next row. P.
Next row. K. to last st. Inc.
Three rows without shaping.
Next row. Cast off 5. K. to last st. K.2 tog.
Three rows without shaping.
Continue as left cheek from ***

(3) Gusset:
Cast on 5. K. in st-st. for 3 ins.
Now inc. in 1st and last st. of every K. row until 19 sts.
Now inc. in 1st and last st. of every 4th row until 23 sts.
K.1½ ins. without shaping, ending with a P. row.
Dec. at beginning and end of next and every 4th row until 15 sts.
Now dec. every K. row until 5 sts.
K.6 rows. Cast off.

Ears (Knit 4)
Cast on 11. K.6 rows. Dec. at beginning and end of next row.
Cast off, knitting 1st 2 sts. and last 2 sts. tog.

Soles (*Knit 2*)
Cast on 4. Inc. at beginning and end of K. rows until 8 sts.
 K.5 rows. K.2 tog. at beginning and end of next row. Cast off.

TO MAKE UP
Sew inner leg seams and then side seams to armholes on wrong side then turn right side out. Run draw thread of matching cotton or invisible nylon thread round bottom of legs and bring them over the soles and sew carefully. The slight gather must be at the front. Push a little stuffing down to the foot and then stitch four claws with brown wool. Continue stuffing until you reach armholes.

 Push a little stuffing right down the arms to hands and make claws with brown wool and continue stuffing arms. Take a couple of stitches at the armhole edge of shoulders and sew in arms, bringing the seam of arm about a quarter of an inch to front of side seams. Now sew rest of shoulder seam. Continue stuffing to neck.

 Fit gusset to cheeks. Cast on edge of gusset to front. Sew on wrong side, taking in cast off stitches of nose in order to give smooth finish. Turn rightside out. Sew each pair of ears on wrong side and turn rightside out. Stuff head firmly making sure the nose is prominent and then make features as in photograph. The eyes are made with satin stitches and a couple of tiny stitches on outer edges with white wool. Now push in more stuffing right to neck edge. Make sure it is very firm or you will have a 'wobbly' head. Run a draw thread round bottom of neck to fit into neck of body. Bring body neck well over and sew firmly. Tie ribbon round neck and sew into position.

DILLY DUCK

Dilly Duck's body (eleven inches) was knitted in two colours, the front yellow the back yellow and blue, the blue coming from top of the head to a point midway down the back. When two colours are used in this way it is necessary to weave the colour not being knitted at the back of the work so that you have no loose loops or loose stitches. This is done by holding the wool not in use in the left hand as for crochet and putting the wool in use over the wool at the back for one stitch and under the wool at the back for the next. For the first two centre stitches in blue it is not necessary to carry the blue wool right along at the back but weave the yellow over it for a couple of stitches on either side to hold it firmly. If the duck is to be made in one colour only the back is knitted exactly the same as the front. If you have not knitted in two colours before it is a good idea to practise with a couple of small balls of wool until you get the hang of it.

MATERIALS

Two balls of 3-ply Angora, one yellow, one blue.

A small ball of 4-ply rust colour for the feet and a small ball of orange 4-ply for the bill. You can use either orange or rust for both if you wish, depending on what you have by you.

Small amount of black for eyes and eyebrows.

Except for wings, stocking-stitch is used throughout but knitted into the back of the stitch on every knit row.

One pair No. 11 needles.

METHOD

Front. Body and head

Cast on 20 stitches.

1st row. K.

2nd row. P.

3rd row. Inc. in 1st st. and last st.

4th row. P.

Continue as 3rd and 4th rows until there are 36 sts. on needle.

Now inc. in every 4th row until there are 50 sts.

K.19 rows without shaping.

K.2 tog. at beginning and end of every 4th row until there are 18 sts.

K.5 rows without shaping.

Inc. at beginning and end of every K. row until there are 26 sts.

11 rows without shaping.

K.2 tog. at beginning and end of every K. row until 20 sts.

K.2 tog. at beginning and end of every row until 6 sts.

Cast off, knitting 2 tog. at beginning and end of cast off row.

Back (if in 2 colours Y = *yellow.* B = *blue)*
K. as for front until there are 50 sts. on needle ending with a P. row.
Next row. K.24 Y. Join in B. K.2 B. K.24 Y.
Next row. P.23 Y. P.4 B. P.23 Y.
Next row. K.22 Y. K.6 B. K.22 Y.
Next row. P.21 Y. P.8 B. P.21 Y.
Continue in this way adding 2 more sts. in blue on every row until the whole of the work is in blue. Fasten off yellow and continue in blue as for front until you reach the last 6 sts. K.2 tog. at beginning and end of every K. row until last st. Draw wool through and fasten off. This gives the point of blue in the front of the head.

Wings
Cast on 20 sts. G-st. throughout.
K.3 ins.
Next row. K.2. K.2 tog. t.b.l. K. to the last 4 sts.
K.2 tog. K.2.
K.7 rows.
Rep. dec. row. (16 sts.)
K. until work measures 5 ins.
Next row. K.8. Put the other 8 sts. on a safety-pin.
K.10 rows on 1st 8 sts.
Next and every row. K.1. K.2 tog. K. to end of row. Continue until 2 sts. remain. K.2 tog. and draw wool through. Rejoin wool and complete second 8 sts. in the same way.
Make another wing.

Feet (st-st. throughout)
Cast on 12.
1st row. K.
2nd row. P.
Inc. at beginning and end of every K. row until 24 sts. Continue without shaping until work measures 2 ins. ending with a P. row.
Next row. Inc. in 1st st. K.11. Leave other 12 sts. on a safety-pin. P. back.
Next row. K. to last 2 sts. K.2 tog.
Next row. P.
Next row. Inc. in 1st st. K. to last 2 sts. K.2 tog.

Next row. P.
Next row. K. to the last 2 sts. K.2 tog.
Continue knitting 2 tog. on the inside of every K. row until all sts. are worked off.
Rejoin wool and make other side but with shapings reversed.
Make another piece in the same way.

Bill (st-st. throughout)
Cast on 10.
K.1 inch ending with a P. row.
Next row. K.2 tog. K. to last 2 sts. K.2 tog.
Next row. P.
Continue dec. at beginning and end of every K. row until 6 sts. remain.
Cast off. knitting 1st 2 sts. and last 2 sts. tog.
Make another piece.

Eyebrows
Cast on 12 sts. in black. K. 2 rows. Cast off.

TO MAKE UP
Sew front and back together bringing blue point neatly on to forehead. Sew two parts of feet on wrong side and turn right side out. Do the same with bill. Stuff body but not too tightly, for angora wool stretches easily and you will spoil the 'cuddly' effect. Sew bottom of duck. Lightly stuff feet and stitch firmly to base. Sew on wings and fold in front. Stitch into position. Arrange eyebrows in loop with cast on edges on the outer side. Make three or four satin-stitches for eyes. Stuff bill and sew into position.

SQUIRREL

MATERIALS
Three ounces of double knitting in golden brown.

Small amount of dark brown 3-ply for nut, features and marking on paws.

Twelve inches of wire for tail.

Binding for tail wire.

Cardboard for winding wool.

Pair of No. 10 knitting-needles and a pair of No. 12.

METHOD

St-st. throughout, knitting into back of stitches on every knit row. Cast on 60 sts. on No. 10 needles.

K.3½ inches.

Next row. K.8. K.2 tog. t.b.l. Rep. to end of row.

K.3 rows.

Next row. K.7. K.2 tog. t.b.l. Rep. to end of row.

K.3 rows.

Next row K.6. K.2 tog. t.b.l. Rep. to end of row.

K.3 rows.

Next row. K.5. K.2 tog. t.b.l. Rep. to end of row.

K.3 rows.

Next row. K.4. K.2 tog. t.b.l. Rep. to end of row.

Change to No. 12 needles and K.8 rows. Change back to No. 10 needles and K.3 rows.

Next row. K.4. Inc. in next st. K.4. Inc. in next st. K.5. Inc. by picking up and knitting loop. K.5. Inc. in next st. K.4. Inc. in next st. K.4. (35 sts.)

Next row. P.

Next row. K.17. K. P. & K. into the next st. (forming 3 sts. from 1 st.) K.17. (37 sts.)

Next row. P.

Next row. Inc. in 1st st. K.17. Pick up loop between last st. and the next and K. K.1. Pick up loop and K. K.17. Inc. in last st. (41 sts.)

Next row. P.

Next row. K.20. Pick up loop and K. K.1. Pick up loop and K. (these centre inc. forms nose) K.20. (43 sts.)

3 rows without shaping.

Next row. K.19. K.2 tog. t.b.l. K.1. K.2 tog. K.19. (41 sts.)

Next row. P.

Next row. K.18. K.2 tog. t.b.l. K.1. K.2 tog. K.18. (39 sts.)

Next row. P.

Next row. K.16. K.3 tog. t.b.l. K.1. K.3 tog. K.16. (35 sts.)
3 rows without shaping.
Next row. K.3. K.2 tog. t.b.l. 3 times. K.5. K.2 tog.
K.3. 3 times. (29 sts.)
Next row. P.
Next row. K.2. K.2 tog. t.b.l. 3 times. K.2 tog. t.b.l. K.1. K.2 tog.
* K.2 tog. K.2. Rep. from * to end of row.
Next row. P.2 tog. 5 times. P.1. P.2 tog. to end of row.
Break off wool. Thread on needle and draw wool through sts. and
fasten into tight circle for top of head. Sew back seam.

Ears (Knit 2)
Cast on 7 sts. on No. 10 needles.
K.4 rows.
Next row. K.2 tog. t.b.l. K.3. K.2 tog.
Next row. P.
Next row. K.2 tog. t.b.l. K.1. K.2 tog. Thread wool through 3 remaining sts. and fasten. Run a thread round edge of ear and gather slightly to curl.

Arms (Knit 2)
Cast on 14 sts. K.2 inches.
Next row. K.2 tog. K. to last 2 sts. K.2 tog.
K.3 rows.
Next row. K.2 tog. K. to last 2 sts. K.2 tog.
Next row. P.
Next row. K.2 tog. to end of row. Thread wool through sts. draw up and fasten off.
Sew seam.

Hind-legs
Cast on 20 sts.
1st row. K. into back of sts.
Next row. P.
Next row. K.2 tog. K. to last st. Inc.
Next row. P.
Next row. K.2 tog. K. to end of row.
Next row. P.
Next row. Cast off 5 sts. K. to last st. Inc.

Next row. P.

Next row. Cast on 3 sts. K. into back of cast on sts. K. to end of row.

Next row. P.

Next row. Inc. in 1st st. K. to last 2 sts. K.2 tog.

3 rows without shaping.

Next row. K.2 tog. K. to last 2 sts. K.2 tog.

Next row. P.

Rep. last 2 rows until 12 sts. remain.

Cast off, knitting 1st 2 sts. tog. and last 2 sts. tog. Make another leg the same.

Make 2 more legs but with the shaping on the purl side. Cast on 20 sts. K. into back of sts. P.1 row. K.1 row.

Next row. P.2 tog. P. to last st. Inc.

Continue as for other sides of legs but reading P. for K.

Base

Cast on 11 sts. P. the 1st row.

Next row. Inc. in 1st st. K. to last. Inc.

Next row. P.

Continue inc. at beginning and end of every other row until 19 sts.

3 rows without shaping.

Now dec. every other row until 11 sts. remain. Cast off.

Nut

Cast on 7 sts. Inc. at begin. and end of every K. row until 13 sts. Now dec. at begin. and end of every K. row until 7 sts. remain. Thread wool through sts. and draw up tightly. Sew seam. Push in a little stuffing and gather cast on edge into circle and fasten off.

Tail

Bend wire at each end into small loop. Bind with strips of nylon or any wool material but as near to the colour of the wool as possible. It must be well padded with the binding or it will be difficult to sew the wool on firmly. Stitch binding securely to loops at each end. Cut a piece of cardboard twelve inches long by one and a half inches wide. Keep back a couple of yards of wool for sewing. Wind the rest of the wool smoothly and evenly over the cardboard. When all the wool is used oversew carefully along one side making sure you catch all strands firmly. Now cut along the other side with a sharp knife. Open wool out and replace cardboard with bound wire. Sew firmly in position right along.

TO MAKE UP

Sew base on to body leaving an opening at back for stuffing. Stuff firmly, a small amount at a time, pushing the nose out carefully as you stuff the head. Sew up base. Embroider eyes with dark brown wool and take needle under to nose. Pinch this out and embroider with satin-stitch and make two stitches for mouth.

Sew ears on either side of head as picture, pulling them forward at tips. Stuff arms and sew to shoulders. Using dark brown wool make stitches for claws. Sew nut to paws. The nut can then be sewn to mouth as picture or just left held by paws.

Sew each pair of hind-legs leaving bottoms open for stuffing. Do not stuff these too tightly. Sew up and then make stitches for claws as on paws. Sew legs on body.

Sew tail at base of body. This must be done so that the wire base is inside the wool. Bend wire slightly so that tail stands away from body then bring back to neck and sew. Curl rest of tail over.

Chapter 9

Alternative Suggestions

Before using any of the patterns it is advisable to recut them on firm paper, marking darts shown and writing clearly which part each pattern is. It is also a good idea to put each pattern in a separate envelope and write the name on the outside. This saves a lot of time later. You can make several patterns of each toy and alter them slightly as described in this chapter.

Suggestions have been made for materials suitable for each toy but there is no need to be rigid about this. Even without altering the shape toys can be varied a great deal by using other materials. Whatever you have by you if the material is strong and the dye fast, use it. This is where cast-off garments come in useful and often the results are far better than you expect. Part of the pleasure is in using what you have to hand. Never use any material that frays easily. The seams will pull and all your work is spoiled.

It has been suggested that the leopard could equally well become a lion, but made in black velvet it becomes a lovely PANTHER. The ears should be pointed and a few strands of fine wool sewn to the tips.

Here are some suggestions for using the patterns in other ways.

Baby Bunny makes a charming BABY BUNTING with very little alteration to the pattern. A face is given for this (Fig. 20). First embroider the face and then cut a circle in the front of bunny's head about a quarter of an inch smaller than the face given. Snip round the edge of the cut circle and turn in all round, tacking lightly. Make a short fringe of wool and stitch under. Insert face into the circle and hem. Sew on three pom-poms as picture. Baby bunting can be made of any material. Strong flowered cotton is excellent. Fur cloth is not quite so easy to handle but is very cuddly.

The baby lamb can be made into a POODLE (see Fig. 21). The nose needs to be cut a little longer and more pointed and the tail should be shorter. A pattern is given for long, floppy ears. The head is improved if about a quarter of an inch is shaped off the back. Material used should

86

Baby Bunting

face   cut 1

FIG. 20.

FIG. 21.
Poodle

be grey, brown or black. Good sateen is the best. Instead of being given just two rows of curls, the back and sides should be covered with them. Make a tuft of wool at the end of the tail and a little tuft under the chin.

The fruity folk can be altered a great deal. The banana man can become a BANANA LADY. The brown piece on the top should be of yellow and dispense with the hat and make long, straight hair of dark brown or black wool and make a short fringe in front (Fig. 22). Use features as for orange senorita. They are so much more feminine. You can add a lace apron which looks quite fetching.

The orange senorita can be made into a fat little APPLE MAN. For this use the banana man's features. Instead of the bun and mantilla make a short plait of green, brown or black wool. The wool needs to be three or four inches long. Plait firmly for about an inch then secure tightly with linen thread. Insert plaited end into top of head and trim to desired length (Fig. 23). A pattern for a waistcoat is given and this can be made in any colour (Fig. 24).

The pattern for Madame Gonk lends itself to many variations in material or colours. If flowered material is used the face may be made separately of plain material and neatly sewn on or inserted as for Baby Bunting. Not that this is a must. If the features are put straight on to the flowered material they are very 'with it'. Or you can make a MR GONK. For this there is no need to make a wig. Just a tuft of hair sticking

FIG. 22. Banana Lady

FIG. 23. Apple Man

a felt waistcoat for apple man   Mr Gonk

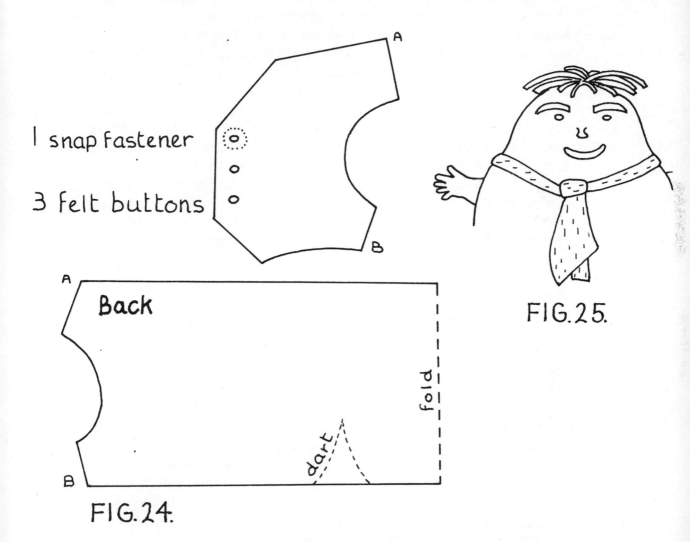

I snap fastener

3 felt buttons

Back

dart

fold

A

B

FIG. 24.

FIG. 25.

up on top as in Fig. 25. Should you prefer a full head of hair it can be made on a base but instead of folding the wool over and stitching it flat it should be opened out and stitched so that it sticks out all over the head. No lace frills are needed but a cuff of straight material may be used instead. It looks just as well without but a tie is a must. This can be a straight piece of material or it can be widened at the ends. You can even make a bow-tie.

The wire people are a good base for 'period' clothes and for this the hair can be altered according to the period. Long hair can be plaited and wound round the head or a bun made at the back. Tiny curls can be made to cover the head and for this the wool needs to be wound round a knitting-needle choosing the size of needle according to the size of the curls required. Another use to which these little people can be put is for fairies on the Christmas tree. For this the shoes should be made as small as possible and in a pastel colour. Layers of net for skirt and sleeves and a folded piece of net or silk for the bodice. Wings can be made of double net and a fine wire sewn round the edges to make them stand out. A silver wand made of wire bound with silver thread can be sewn to one hand. The hair should be made of very fine yellow wool.

Don't be afraid to experiment with glove puppets. Once you have the idea many variations can be made. Using the doll pattern and imagination with the features and it can become a clown. A mop of shaggy hair and a conical hat will complete it. This can be made of any bright material, then stiffened and trimmed with a couple of wool pom-poms.

The monkey pattern can be made into a lovely CLOWN (Fig. 26). Patterns are given for face, boots and hat. Any strong material can be used, the gayer the better. It does not matter if different material is used for arms and legs. The main thing is that it must be strong. Any white, pale pink or yellow material can be used for the face and as the nose and mouth are so simple they need not be made of felt for the edges can be turned in slightly and hemmed on to the face (Fig. 27). The nose is made up on the wrong side, turned rightside out and stuffed before sewing on. The hole into which the face is inserted should be cut slightly larger than that for the monkey. Snip round the edges of the hole cut, turn in neatly and tack before inserting face. The boots may be made of any material but look better if it is not patterned (Fig. 28). They should be made up on the wrong side and then turned rightside out before stuffing. Ears should be inserted one inch lower than for the monkey. The tufts of hair are inserted at the same time as the ears. The arms should be cut one inch shorter. The hat is made in the same way as that for the banana man (Fig. 29). This toy should not be stuffed as tightly as the monkey and no wiring is necessary. If it is intended for a very young child it is better to use no felt apart from the hat and this can be removed when washing the toy is necessary. It is a delightful toy for a two year old.

Children not only need toys but should be encouraged to make them.

Clown

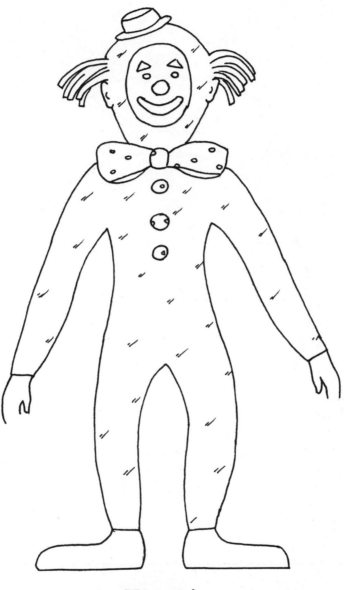

FIG. 26.

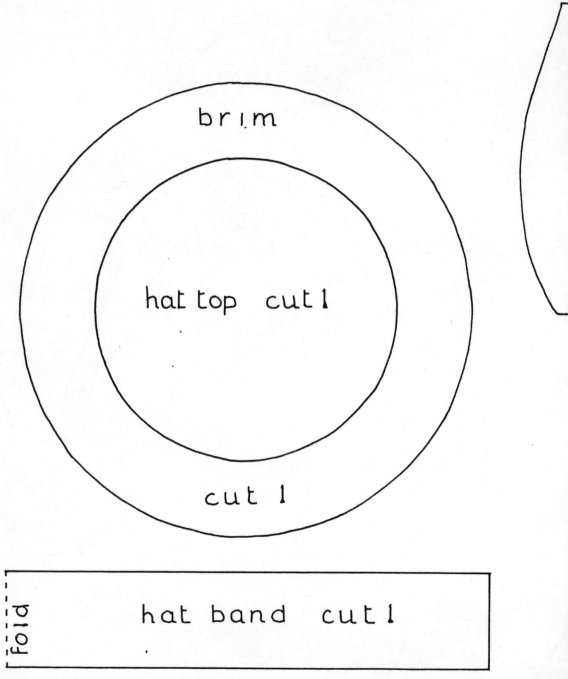

FIG.27. Clown's hat

brim

hat top   cut 1

cut 1

fold

hat band   cut 1

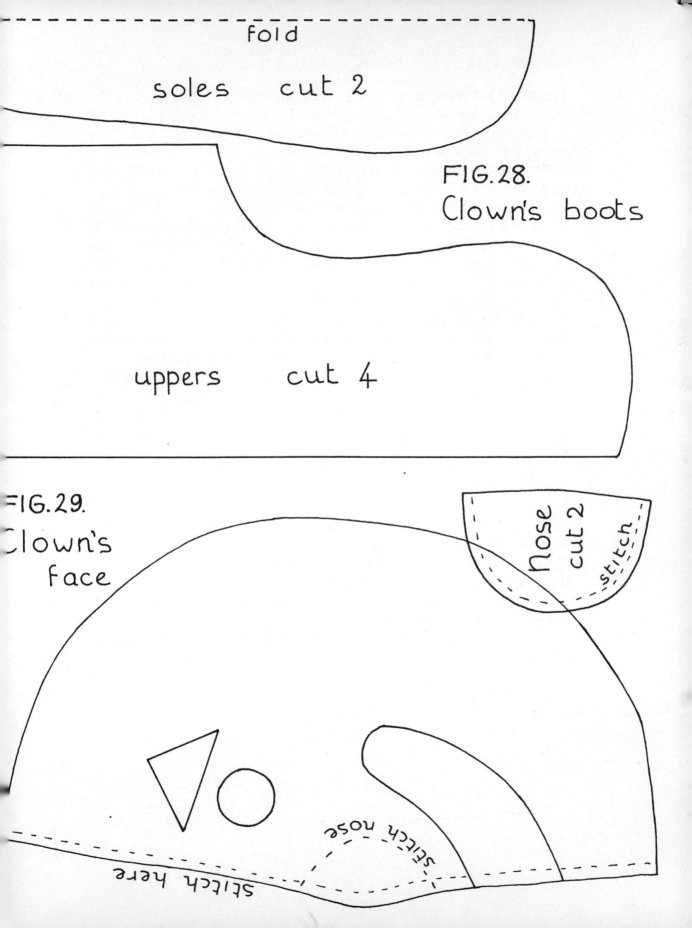

fold

soles   cut 2

FIG.28.
Clown's boots

uppers   cut 4

FIG.29.
Clown's
face

nose
cut 2
stitch

stitch nose

Stitch here

They soon get great fun in making them for younger children either for Christmas or birthday presents. The cat and leopard are simple enough for most children to tackle once they have learned to use a needle. It takes patience to teach a child to sew but it is well worth the effort. Most children take great pleasure in their own handiwork. The results may not be perfect but it is better not to criticize or they may lose heart. They usually see the faults themselves and try to improve.

Modern electric sewing-machines need careful handling but an old-fashioned hand machine is much easier to use. Secondhand ones can often be bought quite cheaply and is a marvellous present for any child who shows an aptitude for sewing. Thank goodness it is no longer considered that only girls should learn to sew and cook. Some of our best dress designers are men as are some of our best chefs. Who knows how quickly a boy may learn to make and design toys! If they want to try they should have every opportunity and encouragement.

Children accumulate toys very quickly and one of the problems is to keep them in some sort of order.

Most children, given the opportunity, consider it part of the fun to arrange their toys for themselves. A low shelf in their own room encourages tidiness.

Another thing which saves hours of clearing up is a small packing case with a lid. This can be covered both inside and out with one of the waterproof, self-adhesive materials such as Contact or Fablon. These are easily wiped over. Children have an aptitude for hoarding and if they have somewhere to store their treasures it saves a great deal of muddle. Bags are an asset and can be made with any odd pieces of material. There should be a drawstring so that it can be pulled up tightly. Bricks, beads, marbles and even pebbles and seashells can be stored in these and are quickly found when needed.

Even tiny children can be taught to be fairly tidy if it is all part of a game.

Useful Tips

USING OLD GARMENTS

1. Unpick first. Wash pieces and press well, discarding parts that have worn thin. Treat lining in same way. This is useful for doll's clothes.

2. Velvet should not be pressed but allowed to drip dry unless a 'crushed velvet' look is wanted. This can be charming but use a cool iron and press on the wrong side.

3. Lace should be unpicked carefully and if there is a gathering thread this should be removed before washing.

4. Jumpers or cardigans which have become matted in the wash will not fray when cut, and make soft, cuddly toys. Small pieces may be used for stuffing along with nylon pieces but not too much wool or the toy will be heavy. Garments of angora or mohair are excellent as they are furry in texture.

5. The wool of hand-knitted garments can be re-knitted. Unpick the seams taking care not to cut through the knitting. Unravel and wind into balls. At this stage the wool is 'kinky' and would make knitting uneven. This is overcome by winding the wool on to a piece of cardboard about fifteen inches by four or five inches. Do not wind tightly. Before taking off cardboard tie hank in several places. These holding pieces should not be tight and it is a good idea to use wool of another colour. Slide hank off cardboard and wash gently in a mild detergent. Roll in a towel and spin dry or press well. Dry thoroughly but not too quickly. Wind into balls. The wool will now knit up as new.

6. Small balls of very fine wool in different colours can be knitted to make mats or carpets for a doll's house. Knit two colours together for best results. Add fringe at each end of mats.

7. The best parts of old towel can be used for toys.

8. If there is no immediate use for these odds and ends it is a good

idea to sort them into groups, spray carefully with a moth-proofing substance and store in clear plastic bags.

USE GOOD TOOLS

1. When sewing, make sure the needle is right for the job. A needle for wool should have an eye large enough to take the strand of wool easily. Always use a fine needle for silk or velvet.

2. Needles, like everything else, wear out. Never use a blunt needle on the machine or when sewing by hand. A blunt needle will pull the threads and spoil the work.

3. Use good knitting needles. Steel, covered with plastic, are far the best. They do not bend easily and do not mark the work if it is left on the needle for a few days.

4. Make sure scissors are really sharp. Blunt scissors pull the material, making it difficult to cut accurately and can also cause a nasty blister on the thumb. It is useful to have three sizes: small embroidery scissors, a middle-sized pair and a pair of tailor's shears.

5. A sharp knife is useful for cutting cardboard and the edges of wool when making hair, fringe or pom-poms. One of the most useful is a linoleum cutter. These can be bought with a steel handle which contains several different types of blades. These can be quickly changed. This piece of equipment needs to be treated with respect and kept well away from children as the blades are very sharp.